Let's Keep in Touch

Follow Us

Visit US at

www.learnpersianonline.com

Call

1-469-230-3605

Online

 www.facebook.com/PersiaClubCo

 www.twitter.com/PersiaClub

 www.instagram.com/LearnPersianOnline

Online Persian Lessons Via Skype

It's easy! Here's how it works.

1- Request a FREE introductory session.

2- Meet a Persian tutor online via Skype.

3- Start speaking Real Persian in Minutes.

Send Email to: **info@LearnPersianOnline.com**

Or Call: **+1-469-230-3605**

www.learnpersianonline.com

... So Much More Online!

- **FREE Farsi lessons**

- **More Farsi learning books!**

- **Online Farsi – English Dictionary**

- **Online Farsi Tutors**

Looking for an Online Farsi Tutor?

Call us at: 001-469-230-3605

Send email to: Info@learnpersianonline.com

Easy Persian

Phrasebook

Essential Expressions for

Communicating in Persian

By

Reza Nazari

ISBN-13: 978-1500115449
ISBN-10: 1500115444

Published by: Learn Persian Online Website

www.learnpersianonline.com

About *Learn Persian Online Website*

The *"Learn Persian Online Website"* was founded on the belief that everyone interested in Persian language should have the opportunity to learn it!

Established in 2012, the *"Learn Persian Online Website"* creates international opportunities for all people interested in Persian language and culture and builds trust between them. We believe in this cultural relations!

If you want to learn more about Persian, this beautiful language and culture, *"Learn Persian Online Website"* is your best starting point. Our highly qualified Persian experts can help you connect to Persian culture and gain confidence you need to communicate effectively in Persian.

Over the past few years, our professional instructors, unique online resources and publications have helped thousands of Persian learners and students improve their language skills. As a result, these students have gained their goals faster. We love celebrating those victories with our students.

Please view our website at:
www.learnpersianonline.com

About the Author

Reza Nazari is a Persian author. He has published more than 50 Persian learning books including:

- Learn To Speak Persian Fast series,
- Farsi Grammar in Use series,
- Persia Club Dictionary Farsi – English,
- Essential Farsi Idioms,
- Farsi Verbs Dictionary
- Read and Write Persian Language in 7 Days
- Laugh and Learn Farsi: Mulla Nasreddin Tales For
    Intermediate to Advanced Persian Learners
- Top 50 Persian Poems of All Time
- Farsi Reading: Improve your reading skill and discover the
    art, culture and history of Iran
- and many more ...

Reza is also a professional Farsi teacher. Over the past eight years, his online Persian lessons have helped thousands of Persian learners and students around the world improve their language skills effectively.

To participate in online Persian classes or ask questions about learning Persian, you can contact Reza via email at: reza@learnpersianonline.com or his Skype ID: rezanazari1

Find Reza's professional profile at:
http://www.learnpersianonline.com/farsi-tutor-reza

Contents

LearnPersianOnline.com

LearnPersianOnline.com

Introduction

Designed as a quick reference and study guide, this comprehensive phrasebook offers guidance for situations including traveling, accommodations, healthcare, emergencies and other common circumstances. A phonetic pronunciation accompanies each phrase and word.

Easy Persian Phrasebook is designed to teach the essentials of Persian quickly and effectively. The common words and phrases are organized to enable the reader to handle day to day situations. The book should suit anyone who needs to get to grips quickly with Persian, such as tourists and business travelers.

Pronunciation Guide

The regular letters used for written Persian stand for some different sounds. It is usually difficult to tell how a word is pronounced just by looking at how it is spelled. Therefore, it is useful to show the pronunciation of each word separately, using a system of symbols in which each symbol stands for one sound only. After each verb in this book, the word is given again within two slashes to show its pronunciation.

This book uses a simple spelling system to show how verbs are pronounced, using the symbols listed below.

Symbol	Example	Symbol	Example
a	hat /hat	m	move /muv
â	cut / cât	n	need /nid
ay	time /tâym	o	gorgeous /gorjes
ch	church /church	ô	coat/ côt
d	dog /dâg	u	mood /mud
e	men /men	p	park /pârk
ey	name /neym	r	rise /rais
f	free /fri	s	seven /seven
g	get /get	sh	shut /shât
h	his /hiz	t	train /treyn
i	feet /fit	v	vary /vari
iyu	cute /kiyut	y	yet /yet
j	jeans /jinz	z	zipper /zipper
k	kettle /ketl	zh	measure /mezher/
kh	loch /lakh	'	تعظیم /ta'zim
l	loss /lâs		

LearnPersianOnline.com

Persian Alphabet

The Persian alphabet (الفبای فارسی) consists 32 letters, most of which have two forms, short and full. It is a writing style based on the Arabic script. The Persian script is entirely written cursively. That is, the majority of letters in a word connect to each other. Some of the letters are similar in shape but differ in the place and number of dots. Some others have the same sound but different shape.

Following is a table showing the Persian alphabet and how it is pronounced in English. There are also some examples of how those letters would sound if you place them in a word.

Row	Letters	Pronunciation	Sample	Pronunciation	Meaning
	آ – ا	**alef**	آب	**āb**	water
1.					
2.	ب – بـ	**be**	بابا	**bābā**	father
3.	پ – پـ	**pe**	پاپ	**pāp**	the pope
4.	ت – تـ	**te**	تاب	**tāb**	swing
5.	ث – ثـ	**se**	اَثاث	**asās**	furniture
6.	ج – جـ	**jim**	تاج	**tāj**	crown
7.	چ – چـ	**che**	چای	**chāi**	tea
8.	ح – حـ	**he**	حَج	**haj**	pilgrimage
9.	خ – خـ	**khe**	خانه	**khāneh**	home
10.	د	**dāl**	دَرد	**dard**	pain
11.	ذ	**zāl**	جَذب	**jazb**	absorption

Row	Letters	Pronunciation	Sample	Pronunciation	Meaning
12.	ر	re	دَر	dar	door
13.	ز	ze	میز	miz	table
14.	ژ	zhe	ژاپُن	zhāpon	japan
15.	س ـ سـ	sin	اُستاد	ostād	professor
16.	ش ـ شـ	shin	دانشجو	dāneshjoo	student
17.	ص ـ صـ	sād	صَد	sad	hundred
18.	ض ـ ضـ	zād	وُضو	vozu	ablution
19.	ط	tā	طَناب	tanāb	rope
20.	ظ	zā	ظُهر	zohr	noon
21.	ع ـ عـ	eyn	عَدَد	adad	number
22.	غ ـ غـ	gheyn	شُغل	shoghl	job

آلفبای فارسی   Farsi Alphabet

	Farsi Alphabet			آلفبای فارسی	
Row	**Letters**	**Pronunciation**	**Sample**	**Pronunciation**	**Meaning**
23.	ف – ف	fe	دَفتَر	daftar	notebook
24.	ق – ق	ghāf	قَهوِه	ghahveh	coffee
25.	ک – ک	kāf	کِتاب	ketāb	book
26.	گ – گ	gāf	دانِشگاه	dāneshgāh	university
27.	ل – ل	lâm	کِلاس	kelās	classroom
28.	مـ – م	mim	مات	māt	blur
29.	نـ – ن	nun	نان	nān	bread
30.	و	vāv	وان	vān	bath
31.	هـ ـه	he	ماه	māh	moon
32.	یـ – ی	ye	نیم	nim	half

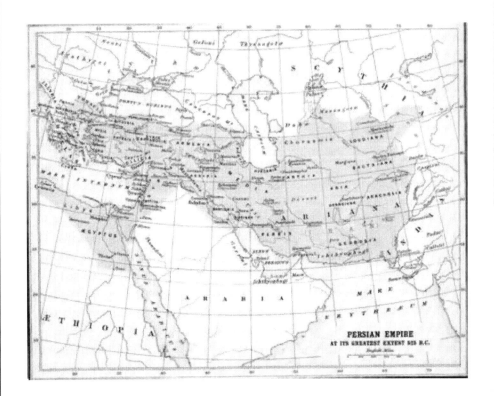

Persian Empire

Quick Reference

مقدماتی

/moghadamâti/

The Basics		مقدماتی /moghadamâti/
English	Pronunciation	Persian
I	man	من
you	to	تو
he , she	u	او
we	mâ	ما
you (formal pl.)	shomâ	شما
they	unâ (ânhâ)	اونا -آنها
it	un	اون
Thank you very much.	kheili mamnun	خیلی ممنونم
Thank you!	mersi	مرسی
You're welcome.	khâhesh mikonam	خواهش می کنم.
Yes	âre - bale	آره - بله
No	kheir - na	خیر - نه
Ladies	khânomhâ	خانم ها
Gentlemen	âghâyân	آقایان
Please	lotfan	لطفاً
I see	midunam - motevaje hastam	می دونم - متوجه هستم
Who?	ki?	کی؟
Why?	cherâ?	چرا؟
What?	chi?	چی؟
When?	key?	کی؟

The Basics		مقدماتی /moghadamâti/
English	**Pronunciation**	**Persian**
Look!	bebin	ببین!
Entrance	vorud	ورود
Exit	khoruj	خروج
I don't understand.	motevaje nemisham	متوجه نمی شم
It's OK.	eshkâli nadâre	اشکالی نداره
How many?	chand tâ?	چند تا؟
How much?	cheghadr?	چقدر؟
How long?	cheghadr tul mikeshe?	چقدر طول می کشه؟
How far?	cheghadr râhe?	چقدر راهه؟
Whom should I ask?	az ki bâyad beporsam?	از کی باید بپرسم؟
After you.	aval shomâ	اول شما
Where is the bathroom?	dastshuyi kojâst?	دستشویی کجاست؟
No smoking	estemâle dokhâniyât mamnu' ast	استعمال دخانیات ممنوع است
Pull	feshâr dahid	فشار دهید
Push	bekeshid	بکشید

Greeting	احوال پرسی /ahvâlporsi/	
English	**Pronunciation**	**Persian**
hello , hi	salâm	سلام
Good afternoon , Good evening	asr bekheyr	عصر بخیر
Good morning.	sobh bekheyr	صبح بخیر
How are you doing?	hâle shomâ chetore?	حال شما چطوره؟
How are you getting along?	ozâ chetore?	اوضاع چطوره؟
It's nice to meet you.	az molâghât bâ shomâ khoshbakhtam	از ملاقات با شما خوشبختم.
goodbye	khodâhâfez	خداحافظ
Good night.	shab bekheir	شب بخیر
See you later.	ba'dan shomâro mibinam	بعداً شما رو می بینم
See you tomorrow.	fardâ shomâ ro mibinam	فردا شما رو می بینم
Take care of yourself.	movâzebe khodetun bâshid	مواظب خودتون باشید
This is my business card.	in kârte vizite mane	این کارت ویزیت منه
This is my telephone number.	in shomâre telefone mane	این شماره تلفن منه
This is my mailing address.	in âdrese mane	این آدرس منه
This is my e-mail address.	in âdrese imeyle mane	این آدرس ایمیل منه

LearnPersianOnline.com

Introductions		معرفی /moarefi/
English	**Pronunciation**	**Persian**
My name is John	esme man jâne	.اسم من جان
What's your name?	esme shomâ chiye?	اسم شما چیه؟
Who are you with?	ki hamrâhetune?	کی همراه تونه؟
I am with my girlfriend.	man bâ dust dokhtaram hastam	.من با دوست دخترم هستم
I am with my family.	man bâ khânevâdam hastam	.من با خانواده م هستم
I am with my children.	man bâ farzandânam hastam	.من با فرزندانم هستم
I am on my own.	man tanhâ hastam	.من تنها هستم
I am with my wife.	man bâ khânomam hastam	.من با خانمم هستم
I am with my fiancée.	man bâ nâmzadam hastam	.من با نامزدم هستم
Where are you from?	ahle kojâyid?	اهل کجایید؟
I am married.	man ezdevâj kardam	.من ازدواج کردم
I am single.	man mojaradam	.من مجردم
I am divorced.	man talâgh gereftam	.من طلاق گرفتم
I am a student.	man daneshjoo hastam	.من دانشجو هستم
I am a manager.	man modiram	من مدیرم
I am a businessman.	man tâjeram	من تاجرم
I am an engineer.	man mohandesam	من مهندسم
I am on vacation.	man barâye ta'tilât	

Introductions		معرفی /moarefi/
English	**Pronunciation**	**Persian**
	umadam	من برای تعطیلات اومدم
I am on business.	man baraye kâr umadam	من برای کار اومدم
I will stay here for a day.	man barâye ye ruz injâ mimunam	من برای یه روز اینجا می مونم
I will stay here for a week.	man barâye ye hafte injâ mimunam	من برای یه هفته اینجا می مونم
I am leaving next week.	man hafteye bad miram	من هفته بعد می رم.
I am leaving next month.	man mâhe bad miram	من ماه بعد می رم.

Jobs		شغل ها /shoghlhâ/
English	**Pronunciation**	**Persian**
Actress, actor	honarpishe	هنر پیشه
Actuary	âmârgir	آمارگیر
Architect	me'mâr	معمار
Archivist	bâyegân	بایگان، ضابط
Army	nezâmi	نظامی
Artist	honarmand	هنرمند
Assistant	dastyâr	دستیار
Babysitter	Parastâre bache	پرستار بچه
Baker	nânvâ	نانوا
Banker	bânkdâr	بانکدار

English	Pronunciation	Persian
	Jobs	شغل ها /shoghlhâ/
Barber	ârâyeshgar	آرایشگر
Blacksmith	âhangar	آهنگر
Boatman	ghâyeghrân	قایقران
Bookseller	ketâbforush	کتاب فروش
Boss	re'is	رئیس
Brigadier	sartip	سر تیپ
Butcher	ghasâb	قصاب
Calligrapher	khatât	خطاط
Cameleer	sârebân	ساربان
Captain	nâkhodâ	نا خدا
Caretaker	serâyedâr	سرایدار
Carpenter	najâr	نجار
Cashier	sandughdâr	صندوقدار
Chef	sarâshpaz	سرآشپز
Clergy man	ruhâni	روحانی
Clerk	kârmand	کارمند
Coach	morabi	مربی (ورزشی)
Colonel	sarhang	سرهنگ
Composer	âhangsâz	آهنگ ساز
Cook	âshpaz	آشپز

Jobs		شغل ها /shoghlhâ/
English	**Pronunciation**	**Persian**
Copilot	komak khalabân	کمک خلبان
Dancer	raghâs	رقاص
Demarche	bakhshdâr	بخشدار
Dentist	dandânpezeshk	دندان پزشک
Detective	kârâgâh	کارگاه
Diplomat	diplomât	دیپلمات
Diver	ghavâs	غواص
Doctor	doktor	دکتر
Doorman	darbân	دربان
Dress maker	khayât	خیاط
Dress maker, tailor	khayât	خیاط
Driver	rânande	راننده
Economist	Eghtesâdd`ân	اقتصاد دان
Editor	virâstâr, sardabir	ویراستار، سر دبیر
Employee	kârmand	کارمند
Employer	kârfarmâ	کارفرما
Engineer	mohandes	مهندس
Farmer	keshâvarz	کشاورز
Firefighter/fireman	âtashneshân	آتش نشان
Fisherman	mâhigir	ماهیگیر

English	Pronunciation	شغل ها /shoghlhâ/ Jobs Persian
flight attendant	mehmândâr	مهماندار
Florist	golforush	گل فروش
Footballer	futbâlist	فوتبالیست
Forester	jangalbân	جنگلبان
Gardener	bâghdâr	باغدار
Glass maker	shishebor	شیشه بر
Governor	farmândâr	فرماندار
Governor	farmândâr	فرماندار
Grocer	baghâl	بقال
Guard	negahbân	نگهبان
Housekeeper	khânedâr	خانه دار
Housekeeper	khânedâr	خانه دار
Hunter	shekârchi	شکارچی
Interpreter	mofarser	مفسر
Jerry builder	besâz befrush	بساز بفروش
Journalist	ruznâmenegâr	روزنامه نگار
Judge	ghâzi	قاضی
Lawyer	vakil	وکیل
Leader	rahbar	رهبر
Maid	khedmatkâr	خدمتکار

Jobs		شغل ها /shoghlhâ/
English	**Pronunciation**	**Persian**
Manager	modir	مدیر
Mason	banâ	بنا
Mayor	shahrdâr	شهردار
Merchant	tâjer	تاجر
Miller	âsiyâbân	آسیابان
Miner	ma'danchi	معدنچی
Minister	vazir	وزیر
Musician	musighidân	موسیقیدان
Nurse	parastâr	پرستار
Officer	afsar	افسر
Operator	telefonchi	تلفنچی
Optician	cheshmpezeshk	چشم پزشک
Optometrist	eynaksâz	عینکساز
Painter	naghâsh	نقاش
Photographer	akâs	عکاس
Physician	pezeshk	پزشک
Pilot	khalabân	خلبان
Player	bâzigar	بازیگر
Plumber	lulekesh	لوله کش
Porter	bârbar	باربر

Jobs		شغل ها /shoghlhâ/
English	**Pronunciation**	**Persian**
Postman	postchi	پستچی
potter	sofâlgar	سفالگر
President	reise jomhur	رئیس جمهور
Priest	keshish	کشیش
Prime minister	nokhostvazir	نخست وزیر
Principal	modire madrese	مدیر مدرسه
Professor	ostâd	استاد
Psychologist	ravanshenâs	روانشناس
Publisher	nâsher	ناشر
Receptionist	monshi	منشی
Referee	dâvar	داور
Repairman	ta'mirkâr	تعمیرکار
Repairman	ta'mirkâr	تعمیرکار
Reporter	gozâreshgar	گزارشگر
Researcher	pazhuheshgar	پژوهشگر
Retired	bâzneshaste	بازنشسته
sailor	malavân	ملوان
scientist	dâneshmand	دانشمند
Sculptor	mojasamesâz	مجسمه ساز
Seafarer	daryânavard	دریا نورد

Jobs		شغل ها /shoghlhâ/
English	**Pronunciation**	**Persian**
Seller	forushande	فروشنده
Sergeant	goruhbân	گروهبان
Shepherd/Rancher	chupân	چوپان
Shepherd/Rancher	chupân	چوپان
Sheriff	kalântar	کلانتر
Shoemaker	kafâsh	کفاش
Shopkeeper	maghâzedâr	مغازه دار
Singer	khânande	خواننده
Soldier	sarbâz	سرباز
Speaker	sokhanrân	سخنران
Specialist	motekhases	متخصص
stockbroker	dalâl	دلال
Street sweeper	roftegar	رفتگر
Student	dâneshâmuz- dâneshju	دانش آموز / دانشجو
Surgeon	jarâh	جراح
Surveyor	naghshe bardâr	نقشه بردار
Teacher	moalem	معلم
Tourist	jahângard	جهانگرد
Translator	motarjem	مترجم
Typist	mâshinevis	ماشین نویس

Jobs		شغل ها /shoghlhâ/
English	**Pronunciation**	**Persian**
Veterinarian	dâmpezeshk	دامپزشک
Waiter	gârson	گارسون
Watchman	sâatsâz	ساعت ساز
Weatherman	havâshenâs	هواشناس
Welder	jushkâr	جوشکار
Worker	kâregar	کارگر
Writer/Author	nevisande	نویسنده

Invitation		دعوت /da'vat/
English	**Pronunciation**	**Persian**
Would you like to meet in the lobby?	dust dâri tu lâbi hamdigaro bebinim?	دوست داری تو لابی همدیگرو ببینیم؟
Do you have free time tomorrow?	fardâ shomâ vaght dârid?	فردا شما وقت دارید؟
Could we see each other today?	mitunim emruz hamdigaro bebinim?	می تونیم امروز همدیگرو ببینیم؟
Do you have free time tonight?	emshab vaghte shomâ âzade?	امشب وقت شما آزاده؟
Whould you like to come with me?	dust dârid bâ man biyâyn?	دوست دارید با من بیاین؟
Do you have any plans for today?	barnâmeye shomâ barâye emruz chiye?	برنامه شما برای امروز چیه؟
Would you like to go for a walk?	dust dârid piyâderavi konim?	دوست دارید پیاده روی

Invitation	دعوت /da'vat/

English	Pronunciation	Persian
		کنیم؟
Would you like to go for a drink?	dust dârid berim nushidani bekhorim?	دوست دارید بریم نوشیدنی بخوریم؟
How would you like to go out for a meal?	dust dârid baraye ghazâ berim birun?	دوست دارید برای غذا بریم بیرون؟
Would you like to go shopping?	dust dârid berim kharid?	دوست دارید بریم خرید؟
I will treat you to a drink.	man shomâ ro be ye nushidani da'vat mikonam	من شما رو به یه نوشیدنی دعوت می کنم.
I don't mind.	mohem nist	مهم نیست.

Praise and Gratitude	تعریف و قدردانی /ta'rif va ghadrdâni/

English	Pronunciation	Persian
That's great.	âliye	عالیه
That's interesting.	jâlebe	جالبه
You look good!	kheili khoshtip shodi!	خیلی خوش تیپ شدی!
What a nice place.	che jâye khubiye	چه جای خوبیه
What a nice view.	che manzareye khubiye	چه منظره خوبیه
Thanks for your trouble.	mamnun az zahmati ke keshidid	ممنون از زحمتی که کشیدید

Praise and Gratitude		تعریف و قدردانی /ta'rif va ghadrdâni/ Persian
English	**Pronunciation**	**Persian**
I enjoyed myself today, thank you.	emruz be man khosh gozasht mersi	امروز به من خوش گذشت، مرسی
Your new haircut is great.	muhât kheili khub shode	موهات خیلی خوب شده
You have wonderful taste in clothes.	shomâ saligheye khubi barâye lebâs dârid	شما سلیقه خوبی برای لباس دارید
That's very kind of you.	vâghean lotf dârid	واقعاً لطف دارید
You're very nice.	shomâ kheili bâ mohabatid	شما خیلی بامحبتید
Much obliged.	kheili mamnunam	خیلی ممنونم
Apologies	mazeratkhâhi	معذرت خواهی
I didn't mean that.	manzuri nadâshtam	منظوری نداشتم
Next time I will get it right.	dafeye bad jobrân mikonam	دفعه بعد جبران می کنم
Sorry I'm late.	bebakhshid ke dir umadam	ببخشید که دیر اومدم
May I bother you for a moment?	mitunam ye lahze mozâhemetun besham?	می تونم یه لحظه مزاحمتون بشم؟
Sorry.	moteasefam	متأسفم
Just a moment please.	lotfan ye deyghe sabr konid	لطفاً یه دیقه صبر کنید
That's my fault.	taghsire mane	تقصیر منه

Requests		درخواستها /darkhâsthâ/
English	**Pronunciation**	**Persian**
Could you please help me?	momkene be man komak konid	ممکنه به من کمک کنید؟
Excuse me, could you please help me?	bebakhshid mitunid be man komak konid?	ببخشید می تونید به من کمک کنید؟
Please repeat that once more	lotfan ye bâr dige tekrâr konid	لطفاً یه بار دیگه تکرار کنید.
Please speak more slowly.	lotfan âhestetar sohbat konid	لطفاً آهسته تر صحبت کنید.
Could you repeat that?	momkene dobâre tekrâr konid?	ممکنه دوباره تکرار کنید؟
Please write it here.	lotfan injâ benevisid	لطفاً اینجا بنویسید.
Do you understand?	bebakhshid motevaje shodid?	ببخشید متوجه شدید؟
Please hurry up.	lotfan ajale konid	لطفاً عجله کنید.
Come with me!	bâ man biyain	با من بیاین!
Could I have your address?	mitunam âdrese shomâ ro dâshte bâsham?	می تونم آدرس شما رو داشته باشم؟
May I have your telephone number?	mitunam shomâreye telefone shomâ ro begiram?	می تونم شماره تلفن شما رو بگیرم؟
May I have your e-mail?	mitunam imeile shomâ ro dâshte bâsham?	می تونم ایمیل شما رو داشته باشم؟

English	Pronunciation	Persian
Could you drop me off downtown?	momkene mano be markaze shahr beresunid?	ممکنه منو به مرکز شهر برسونید؟
Could I take a look at it?	mitunam be in negâhi bendâzam?	می تونم به این نگاهی بندازم؟
May I borrow your pen?	mitunam az khodkâre shomâ estefâde konam?	می تونم از خودکار شما استفاده کنم؟
May I borrow your journal?	mitunam majaleye shomâro gharz begiram?	می تونم مجله شما رو قرض بگیرم؟
Could you please mail this letter for me?	momkene in nâmaro barâye man post konid?	ممکنه این نامه رو برای من پست کنید؟

	احساسات و دعای خیر	
Feelings and Blessing		/ehsâsât va doâye kheyr/
English	**Pronunciation**	**Persian**
That's wonderful!	âliye	عالیه!
That's awful!	eftezâhe!	افتضاحه!
I'm sad	nârâhatam	ناراحتم
I am so excited	kheili hayejân zade hastam	خیلی هیجان زده هستم
I feel bad	hâlam kheili bade	حالم خیلی بده
Calm down, everything will be fine.	ârum bâshid hame chiz dorost mishe	آروم باشید، همه چیز درست می شه.
I'm not sure.	motmaen nistam	مطمئن نیستم.
What a pity!	che bad!	چه بد!

Feelings and Blessing		احساسات و دعای خیر /ehsâsât va doâye kheyr/
English	**Pronunciation**	**Persian**
What a surprise!	che jâleb	چه جالب!
That's enough!	kâfiye!	کافیه!
Of course!	albate!	البته!
Congratulations!	tabrik migam	تبریک میگم!
Merry Christmas!	kerismas mobârak	کریسمس مبارک!
Happy Easter!	eidetun mobârak!	عیدتون مبارک!
Best wishes for a Happy New Year!	behtarin ârezuhâ barâye shâdbâsh sâle no!	بهترین آرزوها برای شادباش سال نو!
Best wishes for your birthday!	behtarin ârezuhâ barâye tavalode shomâ!	بهترین آرزوها برای تولد شما!
Happy Easter!	eyde pâk mobârak!	عید پاک مبارک!
Have a nice trip!	safar khubi dâshte bvshid!	سفر خوبی داشته باشید!
Have a good time!	ôghâte khubi dâshte bâshid!	اوقات خوبی داشته باشید!
Good luck!	movafagh bâshid!	موفق باشید!
Let's meet again!	dobâre hamdigaro mibinim	دوباره همدیگر رو می بینیم
Bon appetite!	nushe jân!	نوش جان!
Enjoy!	khosh begzare!	خوش بگذره!
Cheers!	be salâmati!	به سلامتی!

Weather		آب و هوا /âbo havâ/
English	**Pronunciation**	**Persian**
snow	barf	برف
rain	barun	بارون
sun	khorshid	خورشید
fog	meh	مه
wind	bâd	باد
thunderstorm	tufân - ra'do bargh	توفان - رعد و برق
storm	tufân	توفان
severe weather	havâye bad	هوای بد
heat	garmâ	گرما
How is the weather today?	emruz havâ chetore?	امروز هوا چطوره؟
It's a nice day.	ruze khubiye	روز خوبیه
It's raining.	barun miyâd	بارون میاد
It's snowing.	barf miyâd	برف میاد.
The weather today is good.	emruz havâ khube	امروز هوا خوبه
The weather today is bad.	emruz havâ bade	امروز هوا بده
It's sunny today!	emruz havâ âftâbiye	امروز هوا آفتابیه!
Today it's warm.	emruz havâ garme	امروز هوا گرمه.
Today it's cold.	emruz havâ sarde	امروز هوا سرده.

Time & Dates		زمان و تاریخ /zamân va târikh/
English	**Pronunciation**	**Persian**
What time is it?	sâ'at chande?	ساعت چنده؟
in an hour	ye sâ'ate dige	یه ساعت دیگه
From what time?	az che sâ'ati?	از چه ساعتی؟
Till what time?	tâ che sâ'ati?	تا چه ساعتی؟
It is early.	zude	زوده
It is late.	dire	دیره
It's on time.	be moghe' ast	به موقع است
Is it late?	dire?	دیره؟
It is noon.	zohre	ظهره
It is midnight.	nesfe shabe	نصف شبه
How long will it take?	cheghadr tul mikeshe?	چقدر طول می کشه؟
I am leaving in the morning.	man sobh miram	من صبح میرم
I am leaving in the evening.	man asr miram	من عصر میرم
What day is today?	emruz chand shanbe ast?	امروز چند شنبه است؟
What day is tomorrow?	fardâ chand shanbe ast?	فردا چند شنبه است؟
minute	daghighe	دقیقه
second	sâniye	ثانیه
hour , clock	sâ'at	ساعت
day	ruz	روز

LearnPersianOnline.com

Time & Dates		زمان و تاریخ /zamân va târikh/
English	Pronunciation	Persian
week	hafte	هفته
today	emruz	امروز
yesterday	diruz	دیروز
tomorrow	fardâ	فردا
tomorrow morning	fardâ sobh	فردا صبح
one o'clock	sâ'ate yek	ساعت یک
two o'clock	sâ'ate do	ساعت دو
three o'clock	sâ'ate se	ساعت سه
a.m.	sobh	صبح
p.m.	asr, badazohr	عصر ، بعدالظهر
month	mâh	ماه
January	zhânviye	ژانویه
February	fevriye	فوریه
March	mars	مارس
April	âvril	آوریل
May	mey	می
June	zhuan	ژوئن
July	julây	جولای
August	ut	اوت
September	septâmr	سپتامبر

Time & Dates		زمان و تاریخ /zamân va târikh/
English	**Pronunciation**	**Persian**
October	oktobr	اکتبر
November	novâmr	نوامبر
December	desâmr	دسامبر
Solar Months	mahâye shamsi	ماه های شمسی
March-April	farvardin	فروردین
April-May	ordibehesh	اردیبهشت
May-June	khordâd	خرداد
June-July	tir	تیر
July-August	mordâd	مرداد
August-September	shahrivar	شهریور
September-October	mehr	مهر
October-November	âbân	آبان
November-December	âzar	آذر
December-January	dey	دی
January-February	bahman	بهمن
February-March	esfand	اسفند
year	sâl	سال
spring	bahâr	بهار
summer	tâbestân	تابستان
fall	pâyiz	پاییز

Time & Dates		زمان و تاریخ /zamân va târikh/
English	**Pronunciation**	**Persian**
winter	zemestân	زمستان
Week days	ruzhâye hafte	روزهای هفته
Saturday	shanbe	شنبه
Sunday	yekshanbe	یکشنبه
Monday	doshanbe	دوشنبه
Tuesday	seshanbe	سه شنبه
Wednesday	chârshanbe	چهارشنبه
Thursday	panjshanbe	پنج شنبه

Numbers		اعداد /a'dâd
English	**Pronunciation**	**Persian**
zero	sefr	صفر
one	yek	یک
two	do	دو
three	se	سه
four	chehâr	چهار
five	panj	پنج
six	shesh	شش
seven	haft	هفت
eight	hasht	هشت

Numbers		اعداد /a'dâd
English	**Pronunciation**	**Persian**
nine	noh	نه
ten	dah	ده
eleven	yâzdah	یازده
twelve	davâzdah	دوازده
thirteen	sizdah	سیزده
fourteen	chehârdah	چهارده
fifteen	pânzdah	پانزده
sixteen	shânzdah	شانزده
seventeen	hefdah	هفده
eighteen	hejdah	هجده
nineteen	nuzdah	نوزده
twenty	bist	بیست
twenty-one	bisto yek	بیست و یک
thirty	si	سی
forty	chehel	چهل
fifty	panjâh	پنجاه
sixty	shast	شصت
seventy	haftâd	هفتاد
eighty	hashtâd	هشتاد
ninety	navad	نود

Numbers		اعداد /a'dâd
English	**Pronunciation**	**Persian**
hundred	sad	صد
two hundred	devist	دویست
three hundred	sisad	سیصد
four hundred	chehârsad	چهارصد
five hundred	pânsad	پانصد
Six hundred	sheshsad	ششصد
seven handred	haftsad	هفتصد
eight hundred	hashtsad	هشتصد
nine hundred	nohsad	نهصد
thousand	hezâr	هزار
million	miliyon	میلیون
billion	milyârd	میلیارد

Sports		ورزش ها /varzeshhâ/
English	**Pronunciation**	**Persian**
Badminton	badminton	بدمینتون
baseball	beysbâl	بیسبال
Volleyball	vâlibâl	والیبال
Billiard	biliyârd	بیلیارد
boxing	boks	بوکس

Sports		ورزش ها /varzeshhâ/
English	**Pronunciation**	**Persian**
Swimming	shenâ	شنا
Chess	shatranj	شطرنج
Cricket	keriket	کریکت
Cycling	docharkhe savâri	دوچرخه سواری
Dart	dârt	دارت
Golf	golf	گلف
Gymnastics	zhimnâstik	ژیمناستیک
Hacky	hâki	هاکی
Jogging	do	دو
Soccer	futbâl	فوتبال
Basketball	basketâl	بسکتبال
Wrestling	koshti	کشتی
Karate	kârâte	کاراته
Football	futbâle âmrikâyi	فوتبال آمریکایی

Colors		رنگ ها /ranghâ/
English	**Pronunciation**	**Persian**
Aqua	firuze'i	فیروزه‌ای
Aquamarine	yashmi	یشمی
Bisque	kerem	کرم

Colors		رنگ ها /ranghâ/
English	**Pronunciation**	**Persian**
Black	siyâh	سیاه
Blue	âbi	آبی
Brown	ghahve'i	قهوه‌ای
Coral	bezh	بژ
Crimson	zereshki	زرشکی
Dark Blue	sorme'i	سرمه‌ای
Dark Magenta	makhmali	مخملی
Dim Gray	dudi	دودی
Dodger Blue	nili	نیلی
Fire Brick	sharâbi	شرابی
Goldenrod	khardali	خردلی
Gray	khâkestari	خاکستری
Green	sabz	سبز
Hot Pink	sorkhâbi	سرخابی
Ivory	ostekhâni	استخوانی
Khaki	khâki	خاکی
Light Grey	noghre'i	نقره‌ای
Light Yellow	shiri	شیری
Maroon	âlbâluyi	آلبالویی
Navy	lâjevardi	لاجوردی

Colors		رنگ ها /ranghâ/
English	**Pronunciation**	**Persian**
Olive	zeituni	زیتونی
Orange	nârenji	نارنجی
Orchid	orkide	ارکیده
Pale Goldenrod	nokhodi	نخودی
Pink	surati	صورتی
Purple	arghavâni	ارغوانی
Red	ghermez	قرمز
Salmon	hanâyi	حنایی
Silver	tusi	توسی
Violet	banafsh	بنفش
Wheat	gandomi	گندمی
White	sefid	سفید
Yellow	zard	زرد

Animals		حیوانات /heyvânât/
English	**Pronunciation**	**Persian**
alligator	temsâh	تمساح
anteater	murchekhâr	مورچه خوار
antelope	boze kuhi	بزکوهی
armadillo	gurkan	گورکن
bat	khofâsh	خفاش

Animals		حیوانات /heyvânât/
English	**Pronunciation**	**Persian**
bear	khers	خرس
beaver	sage âbi	سگ آبی
buffalo	gâvmish	گاومیش
buffalo	buffalo	بوفالو
bull	gave nar	گاو نر
calf	gusâle	گوساله
camel	shotor	شتر
cat	gorbe	گربه
cow	gâve made	گاو ماده
crocodile	susmâr	سوسمار
dog	sag	سگ
donkey	olâgh	الاغ
Donkey	khar	خر
elephant	fil	فیل
fox	rubâh	روباه
giraffe	zarâfe	زرافه
goat	boz	بز
gorilla	guril	گوریل
hippo	asbe âbi	اسب آبی
horse	asb	اسب

English	Pronunciation	حیوانات /heyvânât/ Persian
	Animals	
hyena	kaftâr	کفتار
kangaroo	kângoro	کانگورو
kid	bozghâle	بزغاله
koala bear	kulâ	کوالا
lamb	bare	بره
leopard	palang	پلنگ
lion	shir	شیر
mole	mushe kur	موش کور
monkey	meymun	میمون
mouse	mush	موش
mule	ghâter	قاطر
panda	kherse panda	خرس پاندا
pig	khuk	خوک
piglet	bache khuk	بچه خوک
polar bear	kherse ghotbi	خرس قطبی
porcupine	juje tighi	جوجه تیفی
puppy	tule sag	توله سگ
rabbit	khargush	خرگوش
raccoon	râkon	راکون
ram	ghuch	قوچ

حیوانات /heyvânât/	Animals	
English	**Pronunciation**	**Persian**
rat/ vole	mushe sahrâyi	موش صحرایی
sheep	gusfand	گوسفند
skunk	râsu	راسو
snake	mâr	مار
squirrel	sanjâb	سنجاب
tiger	babr	ببر
tortoise	lâkposht	لاک پشت
wolf	gorg	گرگ
zebra	khurekhar	گورخر

حشرات /hasherât/	Insects	
English	**Pronunciation**	**Persian**
Ant	murche	مورچه
Aphid	shate	شته
Bedbug	sâs	ساس
Butterfly	parvâne	پروانه
Cockroach	susk	سوسک
Cricket	jirjirak	جیرجیرک
Damselfly	sanjâghak	سنجاقک
Firefly	kerme shabtâb	کرم شب تاب
Flea	kak	کک

Insects		حشرات /hasherât/
English	**Pronunciation**	**Persian**
Fly	magas	مگس
Grasshopper	malakh	ملخ
Honey bee	zanbure asal	زنبور عسل
Lacewing	baltori	بالتوری
Ladybird beetle	pineduz	پینه دوز
Maggot	kerme hashare	کرم حشره
Mosquito	pashe	پشه
Praying mantis	âkhundak	آخوندک
Queen bee	malakeye zanbure asal	ملکه زنبور عسل
Termite	muriyâne	موریانه
Wasp	zanbur	زنبور

Flowers		گل ها /golhâ/
English	**Pronunciation**	**Persian**
Bougainvillea	gole kâzhazi	گل کاغذی
Buttercup	âlâle	آلاله
Cactus	kâktus	کاکتوس
Carnation	mikhak	میخک
Daffodil	narges	نرگس
Dahlia	kokab	کوکب

Flowers		گل ها /golhâ/
English	Pronunciation	Persian
daisy	gole morvârid	مروارید
Damascus rose or Damask rose	mohamadi	محمدی
Dandelion	ghâsedak	قاصدک
Fox gloves	angoshtâne	انگشتانه
Freesia	feriziyâ	فریزیا
Geranium	shamdâni	شمعدانی
Hollyhock	khatmi	ختمی
iris	susan-zanbagh	سوسن-زنبق
ivy	pichak	پیچک
Jonquil	nastaran	نسترن
Marguerite	dâvudi-minâ	داوودی-مینا
Oleander	kharzare	خرزهره
Orchid	orkide	ارکیده
Pansy	banafsheye farangi	بنفشهءفرنگی
Red bud	arghavân	ارغوان
sedum	gole nâz	گل ناز
Silk tasseled	abrisham	ابریشم
Sizing	âhâr	آهار
Snap dragon	gole meimun	میمون

Flowers		گل ها /golhâ/
English	**Pronunciation**	**Persian**
Snowdrop	gole yakh	گل یخ
Sun flower	âftâbgardân	اَفتابگردان
Tuberose	maryam	مریم
Tulip	lâle	لاله

Body		اعضای بدن /a'zâye badan/
English	**Pronunciation**	**Persian**
ankle	ghuzake pâ	قوزک پا
arm	bâzu	بازو
back	posht	پشت
beard	rish	ریش
breast	sine	سینه
Chin	châne	چانه
Ear	gush	گوش
elbow	ârenj	آرنج
Eye	cheshm	چشم
Eyebrow	abru	ابرو
Eyelash	mozhe	مژه
Finger/Foe	angosht	انگشت

English	Pronunciation	اعضای بدن /a'zâye badan/ Persian
	Body	
Forehead	pishâni	پیشانی
Hair	mu	مو
Hand	dast	دست
Head	sar	سر
Heart	ghalb	قلب
intestine	rude	روده
knee	zânu	زانو
Leg	pâ	پا
Lungs	shosh	شش
Mouth	dahân	دهان
mustache	sebil	سبیل
nail	nâkhon	ناخن
navel	nâf	ناف
Neck	garden	گردن
Nose	damâgh	دماغ
palms	kafe dast	کف دست
penis	âlate tanâsoli	آلت تناسلی
Shoulder	shâne	شانه
Stomach	shekam	شکم
stomach	me'de	معده

Body		اعضای بدن /a'zâye badan/
English	Pronunciation	Persian
teeth	dandân	دندان
wrist	moche dast	مچ دست

Countries, Nationality & Languages

کشورها، ملیتها و زبانها

/keshvarhâ, meliyathâ va zabânhâ/

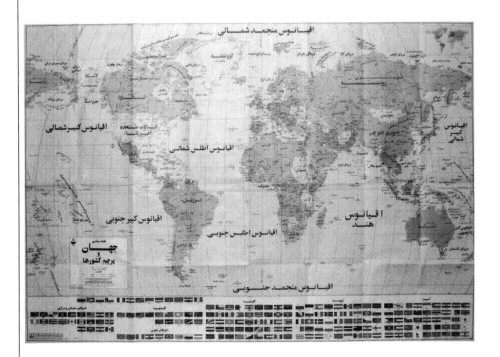

Countries		کشورها /keshvarhâ/
English	**Pronunciation**	**Persian**
Afghanistan	afghânestan	افغانستان
Argentina	ârzhantin	آرژانتین
Australia	osterâliâ	استرالیا
Austria	otrish	اتریش
Belgium	belzhik	بلژیک
Bolivia	bolivi	بلیوی
Brazil	berezil	برزیل
Cambodia	kâmboj	کامبوج
Canada	kânâdâ	کانادا
Chile	shili	شیلی
China	chin	چین
Colombia	kolombiâ	کلمبیا
Costa Rica	kâstârikâ	کاستاریکا
Cuba	kubâ	کوبا
Denmark	dânmârk	دانمارک
Dominican Republic	jomhuriye dominikan	جمهوری دومینیکن
Ecuador	ekvâdor	اکوادور
Egypt	mesr	مصر
El Salvador	elsâlvâdor	السالوادور
England	engelestân	انگلستان

Countries		کشورها /keshvarhâ/
English	**Pronunciation**	**Persian**
Estonia	estoni	استونی
Ethiopia	etiyupi	اتیوپی
Finland	fanlând	فنلاند
France	farânse	فرانسه
Germany	âlmân	آلمان
Greece	yunân	یونان
Guatemala	goâtmâlâ	گواتمالا
Haiti	hâyiti	هائیتی
Honduras	hendorâs	هندوراس
Hungary	majârestân	مجارستان
Indonesia	andonezi	اندونزی
Iran	irân	ایران
Ireland	irland	ایرلند
Italy	itâliyâ	ایتالیا
Japan	zhâpon	ژاپن
Jordan	ordon	اردن
Korea	kore	کره
Laos	lâos	لائوس
Latvia	letoni	لتونی
Lithuania	litvâni	لیتوانی

Countries		كشورها /keshvarhâ/
English	**Pronunciation**	**Persian**
Malaysia	mâlezi	مالزی
Mexico	mekzik	مکزیک
Morocco	marâkesh	مراکش
Netherlands	holand	هلند
New Zealand	niyuzland	نیوزلند
Nicaragua	nikârâgue	نیکاراگوئه
Norway	norvezh	نروژ
Panama	panama	پاناما
Paraguay	pârâgue	پاراگوئه
Peru	peru	پرو
Philippines	filipin	فیلیپین
Poland	lahestân	لهستان
Portugal	porteghâl	پرتغال
Puerto Rico	porteriko	پرتریکو
Romania	români	رومانی
Russia	rusiye	روسیه
Saudi Arabia	arabestâne so'udi	عربستان سعودی
Spain	espâniyâ	اسپانیا
Sweden	sued	سوئد
Switzerland	suis	سوئیس

Countries		كشورها /keshvarhâ/
English	**Pronunciation**	**Persian**
Taiwan	tâyvân	تایوان
Thailand	tâland	تایلند
Turkey	torkiye	ترکیه
Ukraine	okrâyn	اکراین
United States	âmrikâ	آمریکا
Uruguay	orugue	اروگوئه
Venezuela	venezuelâ	ونزوئلا
Vietnam	vietnâm	ویتنام
Wales	velz	ولز

Nationality		ملیت ها /meliyathâ/
English	**Pronunciation**	**Persian**
Afghan	afghâni	افغانی
American *	âmrikâyi	آمریکایی
Argentine / Argentinean	ârzhantini	آرژانتینی
Australian	osterâliâyi	استرالیایی
Austrian	otrishi	اتریشی
Belgian	belzhiki	بلژیکی
Bolivian	boliviyâyi	بلیویایی
Brazilian	berezili	برزیلی

Nationality		ملیت ها /meliyathâ/
English	Pronunciation	Persian
Cambodian	kâmboji	کامبوجی
Canadian	kânâdâyi	کانادایی
Chilean	shiliyâyi	شیلیایی
Chinese	chini	چینی
Colombian	kolombiâyi	کلمبیایی
Costa Rican	kâstârikâyi	کاستاریکایی
Cuban	kubâyi	کوبایی
Danish (Dane)	dânmârki	دانمارکی
Dominican	ahle jomhuriye dominikan	اهل جمهوری دومینیکن
Dutch	holandi	هلندی
Ecuadorian	ekvâdori	اکوادوری
Egyptian	mesri	مصری
English	engelisi	انگلیسی
Estonian	estoniyâyi	استونیایی
Ethiopian	etiyupiyâyi	اتیوپیایی
Filipino	filipini	فیلیپینی
Finnish	fanlândi	فنلاندی
French	farânsavi	فرانسوی
German	âlmâni	آلمانی
Greek	yunâni	یونانی

Nationality	ملیت ها /meliyathâ/	
English	**Pronunciation**	**Persian**
Guatemalan	goâtmâlâyi	گواتمالایی
Haitian	ahle hâyiti	اهل هائیتی
Honduran	hendorâsi	هندوراسی
Hungarian	majârestâni	مجارستانی
Indonesian	andoneziâyi	اندونزیایی
Iranian	irâni	ایرانی
Irish	irlandi	ایرلندی
Italian	itâliyâyi	ایتالیایی
Japanese	zhâponi	ژاپنی
Jordanian	ordoni	اردنی
Korean	kore'i	کره ای
Laotian	lâosi	لائوسی
Latvian	letoniyâyi	لتونیایی
Lithuanian	litvâni	لیتوانیایی
Malaysian	mâleziyâyi	مالزیایی
Mexican	mekziki	مکزیکی
Moroccan	marâkeshi	مراکشی
New Zealander	niyuzlandi	نیوزلندی
Nicaraguan	nikârâgue'i	نیکاراگوئه ای
Norwegian	norvezhi	نروژی

Nationality		ملیت ها /meliyathâ/
English	**Pronunciation**	**Persian**
Panamanian	panamayi	پانامایی
Paraguayan	pârâgue'i	پاراگوئه ای
Peruvian	peruyi	پرویی
Polish	lahestâni	لهستانی
Portuguese	porteghâli	پرتغالی
Puerto Rican	porterikoyi	پرتریکو یی
Romanian	româniyâyi	رومانیایی
Russian	rusiye'i	روسیه ای
Salvadorian	elsâlvâdori	السالوادوری
Saudi	ahle arabestâne so'udi	اهل عربستان سعودی
Spanish	espâniyâyi	اسپانیایی
Swedish	suedi	سوئدی
Swiss	suisi	سوئیسی
Taiwanese	tâyvâni	تایوانی
Thai	tâlandi	تایلندی
Turkish	torkiye'i	ترکیه ای
Ukrainian	okrâyni	اکراینی
Uruguayan	orugue'i	اروگوئه ای
Venezuelan	venezuelâyi	ونزوئلایی
Vietnamese	vietnâmi	ویتنامی

Nationality		ملیت ها /meliyathâ/
English	Pronunciation	Persian
Welsh	velzi	ولزی

Languages		زبان ها /zabânhâ/
English	Pronunciation	Persian
Amharic	amhari	امهری
Arabic	arabi	عربی
Cambodian	kâmboji	کامبوجی
Chinese	chini	چینی
Danish	dânmârki	دانمارکی
Dari (Persian)	dari	دری
Dutch	holandi	هلندی
English	ingilisi	انگلیسی
Estonian	estoniyâyi	استونیایی
Farsi (Persian)	fârsi	فارسی
Finnish	fanlândi	فنلاندی
French	farânsavi	فرانسوی
German	âlmâni	آلمانی
Greek	yunâni	یونانی
Hungarian	majârestâni	مجارستانی
Indonesian	andoneziâyi	اندونزیایی

Languages		زبان ها /zabânhâ/
English	**Pronunciation**	**Persian**
Italian	itâliyâyi	ایتالیایی
Japanese	zhâponi	ژاپنی
Korean	kore'i	کره ای
Laotian	lâosi	لائوسی
Latvian	letoniyâyi	لتونیایی
Lithuanian	litvâni	لیتوانیایی
Malay	mâleziyâyi	مالزیایی
Norwegian	norvezhi	نروژی
Polish	lahestâni	لهستانی
Portuguese	porteghâli	پرتغالی
Romanian	româniyâyi	رومانیایی
Russian	rusi	روسی
Spanish	espâniyâyi	اسپانیایی
Swedish	suedi	سوئدی
Tagalog	filipini	فیلیپینی
Thai	tâlandi	تایلندی
Turkish	torki	ترکی
Ukrainian	okrâyni	اکراینی
Vietnamese	vietnâmi	ویتنامی
Welsh	velzi	ولزی

Traveling

مسافرت

/mosâferat/

Booking		رزرو
		/rezerv/
English	**Pronunciation**	**Persian**
How can I get to this place from here?	chetor mitunam az injâ be in mahal beram?	چطور می تونم از اینجا به این محل برم؟
Is that a direct flight?	in parvâz yeksare hast?	این پرواز یکسره هست؟
Is that a non-stop flight?	in parvâz bedune tavaghofe?	این پرواز بدون توقفه؟
Is that an express train?	in ghatâre sario seyre?	این قطار سریع السیره؟
Are there any seats on the flight?	tu parvâz jâye khâkli hast?	تو پرواز جای خالی هست؟
Are there any seats on the train?	tu ghatâr jâye khâli hast?	تو قطار جای خالی هست؟
Are there any seats on the bus?	tu otobus jâye khâli hast?	تو اتوبوس جای خالی هست؟
How frequent are the flights?	har chand vaght yekbâr parvâz hast?	هر چند وقت یکبار پرواز هست؟
How frequent are the trains?	har chand vaght yekbâr ghatâr hast?	هر چند وقت یکبار قطار هست؟
How frequent are the buses?	har chand vaght yekbâr otobus hast?	هر چند وقت یکبار اتوبوس هست؟
Do I have to change planes?	bâyad havâpeimâ avaz konam?	باید هواپیما عوض کنم؟
Do I have to change trains?	bâyad ghatâr avaz konam?	باید قطار عوض کنم؟

I would like to reserve a seat on this plane.	man mikhâm ye jâ tu in parvâz rezerv konam	من می خوام یه جا در این پرواز رزرو کنم.
I would like to reserve a seat on this train.	man mikhâm ye jâ dar in ghatâr rezerv konam	من می خوام یه جا در این قطار رزرو کنم.
I would like to reserve a seat on this bus.	man mikhâm ye jâ dar in otobus rezerv konam	من می خوام یه جا در این اتوبوس رزرو کنم.
How much is the ticket?	gheimate belit chande?	قیمت بلیط چقدره؟
Are there any reduced fares?	gheimate pâyintari nist?	قیمت پایین تری نیست؟
Two business class ticket, please.	do tâ bilite bezines kelâs lotfan	دوتا بلیط بیزینس کلاس لطفاً.
"One economy class ticket, please."	ye bilite ekonomi kelâs lotfan	یث بلیط اکانومی کلاس لطفاً.
"A round-trip ticket, please."	ye bilite rafto bargasht lotfan	یه بلیط رفت و برگشت لطفاً.
"A one-way ticket, please."	ye bilite yeksare lotfan	یه بلیط یکسره لطفاً.
How early must I be at the airport?	cheghadr zudtar bâyad forudgâh bâsham?	چقدر زودتر باید فرودگاه باشم؟
How early must I be at the station?	cheghadr zudtar bâyad tu istgâh bâsham?	چقدر زودتر باید تو ایستگاه باشم؟
What time do I have to check in?	che sâati bâyad barâye savâr shodan eghdâm konam?	چه ساعتی باید برای سوار شدن اقدام کنم؟

English	Pronunciation	Persian
What time does the flight leave?	che sâati parvâz harkat mikone?	چه ساعتی پرواز حرکت می کنه؟
What time does the train leave?	che sâati ghatâr harkat mikone?	چه ساعتی قطار حرکت می کنه؟
What time does the bus leave?	che sâati otobus harkat mikone?	چه ساعتی اتوبوس حرکت می کنه؟
What time will we arrive?	che sâati miresim?	چه ساعتی می رسیم؟
How much baggage can I take?	cheghadr bâr mitunam dâshte bâsham?	چقدر بار می تونم داشته باشم؟
I don't have any baggage.	man bâri nadâram	من باری ندارم.
I would like to cancel my reservation.	man mikhâm rezervamo bâtel konam	من می خوام رزروم رو باطل کنم.
I would like to change my reservation.	man mikhâm rezervamo taghir bedam	من می خوام رزروم رو تغییر دهم.
I would like to confirm my reservation.	man mikhâm rezervamo ta'yid konam	من می خوام رزروم رو تأیید کنم.

Flight Registration		ثبت برای پرواز
		sabt barâyr parvâz
English	Pronunciation	Persian
Excuse me, where is the Lufthansa counter?	bebakhshid bâjeye luftanzâ kojâst?	ببخشید باجه لوفتانزا کجاست؟
Where do I check in?	kojâ bâyad kârte parvâz begiram?	کجا باید کارت پرواز بگیرم؟

Flight Registration		ثبت برای پرواز sabt barâyr parvâz
English	**Pronunciation**	**Persian**
		بگیرم؟
"Send my baggage to the hotel, please."	lotfan chamedunâye mano be hotelam befrestid	لطفاً چمدونای منو به هتلم بفرستید.
How much is the excess baggage charge?	hazineye ezâfe bâr cheghadre?	هزینه اضافه بار چقدره؟
When does boarding begin?	savâr kardane mosâferan key shoru mishe?	سوار کردن مسافران کی شروع می شه؟
Arrivals	parvâz haye vorudi	پروازهای ورودی
Departures	parvâz hâye khoruji	پروازهای خروجی
security check	bâzresiye amniyati	بازرسی امنیتی
passport control	kontorole gozarnâme	کنترل گذرنامه
gate	geyt	گیت
delayed	takhir dâre	تأخیر دارد
landed	be zamin neshast	به زمین نشست
canceled	laghv shod	لغو شد
flight	parvâz	پرواز
flight number	shomâreye parvâz	شماره پرواز
What gate does this flight leave from?	parvâz az kodum geyte?	پرواز از کدوم گیته؟

Will this flight leave on time?	in parvâz ra'se sâat harkat mikone?	این پرواز رأس ساعت حرکت می کنه؟
Are there any delays?	takhir dare?	تأخیر داره؟
I would like a window seat, please.	lotfan ye sandali kenâre panjare be man bedid.	لطفاً یه صندلی کنار پنجره به من بدید.
I would like an aisle seat, please.	loftan ye sandali kenâre râhro be man bedid	لطفاً یه صندلی کنار راهرو به من بدید.
Can we do some shopping in the airport?	mitunim tu forudgâh kharid konim?	می تونیم تو فرودگاه خرید کنیم؟
What currency is this in?	be che puliye?	به چه پولیه؟
Can I pay in euros?	mitunam bâ yoro pardâkht konam?	می تونم با یورو پرداخت کنم؟
Can I pay in traveler's checks?	mitunam bâ cheke mosâferati pardâkht konam?	می تونم با چک مسافرتی پرداخت کنم؟
Do I have to pay duty on the goods I bought here?	bâyad barâye chizâyi ke injâ kharidam gomroki bedam?	باید برای چیزایی که اینجا خریدم گمرگی بدم؟
Please give me a receipt.	lotfan be man resid bedid	لطفاً به من رسید بدید.

On the plane		در هواپیما dar havâpeymâ
English	**Pronunciation**	**Persian**
Where is this seat?	in sandali kojâst?	این صندلی کجاست؟
May I change seats with you?	momkene jâmo bâ shomâ avaz konam?	ممکنه جامو با شما عوض کنم؟
Could you please get me a pillow?	momkene ye bâlesh barâye man begirid	ممکنه یه بالش برای من بگیرید؟
An air sickness bag, please.	lotfan ye kiseye estefrâgh be man bedid	لطفاً یه کیسه استفراغ به من بدید.
Please give me a bottle of beer.	lotfan ye botri âbjo be man bedid	لطفاً یه بطری آبجو به من بدید.
Please give me a glass of wine.	lotfan ye livân sharâb be man bedid	لطفاً یه لیوان شراب به من بدید.
Could I have another drink?	momkene ye nushidaniye dige be man bedid?	ممکنه یه نوشیدنی دیگه به من بدید؟
I want to order some drinks.	man mikhâm nushidani sefâresh bedam	من می خوام نوشیدنی سفارش بدم.
I would like to order something to eat.	man mikhâm ghazâ sefâresh bedam	من می خوام غذا سفارش بدم.
I would like some tea, please.	man chây mikhâm lotfan	من چای می خوام، لطفاً.
I would like some coffee, please.	man ghahve mikhâm lotfan	من قهوه می خوام، لطفاً.
How long will it be delayed?	cheghadr ta'khir dâre?	چقدر تأخیر داره؟

On the plane		در هواپیما dar havâpeymâ
English	**Pronunciation**	**Persian**
When will the flight leave?	havâpeymâ key boland mıshe?	هواپیما کی بلند می شه؟
When will the flight arrive?	havâpeymâ key mishine?	هواپیما کی می شینه؟
How long will we stop here?	che modat injâ tavaghof dârim?	چه مدت اینجا توقف داریم؟
I feel sick.	hâlam khub nist	حالم خوب نیست.
Could I recline my seat?	momkene poshte sandalim ro bekhâbunam?	ممکنه پشت صندلیم رو بخوابونم؟
Fasten seat belts.	kamarbandhâye khod râ bebandid	کمربندهای خود را ببندید.
oxygen mask	mâske oksizhen	ماسک اکسیژن
lavatory	dastshuyi	دستشویی

Train/ Bus/ Boat		قطار/اتوبوس/قایق ghatâr / otobus/ ghâyegh
English	**Pronunciation**	**Persian**
Could I have a schedule?	momkene ye barnâmeye harkat be man bedid?	ممکنه یه برنامه حرکت به من بدید؟
Is this bus schedule current?	in barnâmeye harkate fe'liye otobuse?	این برنامه حرکت فعلی اتوبوسه؟

Is this train schedule current?	in barnâmeye harkate fe'liye ghatâre?	این برنامه حرکت فعلی قطاره؟
I missed the bus. When does the next one depart?	man otobus ro az dast dâdam. ba'di kei harkat mikone?	من اتوبوس رو از دست دادم. بعدی کی حرکت می کنه؟
Is this a direct train?	in ghatâr mostaghime?	این قطار مستقیمه؟
Is there a dining car?	tu ghatâr vâgone resturân hast?	تو قطار واگن رستوران هست؟
Which car is my seat in?	jâye man tu kodum vâgone?	جای من تو کدوم واگنه؟
Where is my seat?	jâye man kojâst?	جای من کجاست؟
Where is my compartment?	kupeye man kojâst?	کوپه من کجاست؟
Is this seat occupied?	injâ jâye kasiye?	اینجا جای کسیه؟
I think this is my seat.	fekr mikonam injâ jâye mane	فکر می کنم اینجا جای منه
How long does the train stop here?	ghatâr cheghadr injâ tavaghof dâre?	قطار چقدر اینجا توقف داره؟
How long does the bus stop here?	otobus cheghadr injâ tavaghof dâre?	اتوبوس چقدر اینجا توقف داره؟
Where is the next stop?	tavaghofe ba'di kojâst?	توقف بعدی کجاست؟
Which stop should I get off at?	kodum istgâh bâyad piyâde besham?	کدوم ایستگاه باید پیاده بشم؟
Stop here, please.	lotfan injâ beistid	لطفاً اینجا بایستید.

How many stops from here?	chand istgâh az injâ?	چند ایستگاه از اینجا؟
luggage rack	jâye asâsiyeye mosâfer	جای اثاثیه مسافر
compartment	kupe	کوپه
car	vâgon	واگن
destination	maghsad	مقصد
departure time	zamâne harkat	زمان حرکت
track	khate râh âhan	خط راه آهن
waiting room	sâlone entezâr	سالن انتظار
To the platforms	be samte sakuhâ	به سمت سکوها
lost-and-found office	daftare ashyâ'e peidâ shode	دفتر اشیاء پیدا شده
Emergency brake	tormoze ezterâri	ترمز اضطراری
alarms	âzhir	آژیر
request stop	darkhâste tavaghof	درخواست توقف
night bus	otobuse shabâne	اتوبوس شبانه
Boat	ghâyegh	قایق
Where is the dock?	bârandâz kojâst?	بار انداز کجاست؟
Where can I board the ship?	kojâ mitunam savâre keshti besham?	کجا می تونم سوار کشتی بشم؟
What time does the ship sail?	keshti che sâati râh miyofte?	کشتی چه ساعتی راه می افته؟
What time does the ship land?	keshti che sâati pahlu migire?	کشتی چه ساعتی پهلو می گیره؟

Would you please show me to my cabin?	momkene lotfan kabinamo neshunam bedid	ممکنه لطفاً کابینمو نشونم بدید
No access to car decks	vorud be arshe makhsuse mâshinhâ mamnu' ast	ورود به عرشه مخصوص ماشینها ممنوع است
lifeboat	ghâyeghe nejât	قایق نجات
life vest	jaligheye nejât	جلیقه نجات
cabin	kâbin	کابین
deck	arshe	عرشه
upper deck	arsheye bâlâ	عرشه بالا
lower deck	arsheye pâyin	عرشه پایین
Baggage	asâsiyeye mosâfer	اثاثیه مسافر
Where can I get my baggage?	az kojâ mitunam asâsiam ro begiram?	از کجا می تونم اثاثیه ام رو بگیرم؟
I can't find my baggage.	man nemitunam asâsiyam ro peidâ konam	من نمی تونم اثاثیه ام رو پیدا کنم.
I didn't receive the claim tag when I checked in.	vaghti asâsiyam ro tahvil dâdam resid nagereftam	وقتی اثاثیه ام رو تحویل دادم رسید نگرفتم.
"My baggage is broken, and some things are missing."	vasâyele man shekaste va bazi chizhâye man gom shode	وسایل من شکسته و بعضی چیزهای من گم شده
This is my baggage.	in asâsiyeye mane	این اثاثیه منه
Where are the luggage lockers?	sandoghhâye asâsiyeye kojâst?	صندوق های اثاثیه کجاست؟

English	Pronunciation	Persian
Where are the luggage carts?	charchdastihâye bâr kojâst?	چرخ دستی های بار کجاست؟

Taxi		تاکسی / tâksi /
English	**Pronunciation**	**Persian**
Where is a taxi stand?	istgâhe tâksi kojâst?	ایستگاه تاکسی کجاست؟
Would you call a taxi for me, please?	momkene barâye man ye tâksi sedâ konid?	ممکنه برای من یه تاکسی صدا کنید؟
I would like a taxi now.	man hamin hâlâ tâksi mikhâm	من همین حالا تاکسی می خوام.
I would like a taxi in an hour.	man ye sâat dige tâksi mikhâm	من یه ساعت دیگه تاکسی می خوام.
Are you free?	vaght darid?	وقت دارید؟
Take me downtown, please.	lotfan mano be markaze shahr bebarid	لطفاً منو به مرکز شهر ببرید.
How much will it cost to go to the airport?	kerâye tâ forudgâh chande?	کرایه تا فرودگاه چنده؟
How much will it cost to go to the train station?	kerâye tâ istgâhe ghatâr chande?	کرایه تا ایستگاه قطار چنده؟
Take me to the airport, please.	lotfan mano be forudgâh bebarid	لطفاً منو به فرودگاه ببرید.
Take me to this hotel, please.	lotfan mano be in hotel bebarid	لطفاً منو به این هتل ببرید.
Take me there, please.	lotfan mano unjâ bebarid	لطفاً منو اونجا ببرید.

Taxi		تاکسی
		/ tâksi /
English	**Pronunciation**	**Persian**
Too much.	kheili ziyâde	خیلی زیاده
The most direct route.	mostaghimtarin masir	مستقیم ترین مسیر.
Slow down.	sor'ate mashin ro kam konid	سرعت ماشین رو کم کنید.
To the right.	be râst	به راست.
To the left.	be chap	به چپ.
Stop here.	injâ be'istid	اینجا بایستید.
Can you wait?	mitunid montazer bemunid?	می تونید منتظر بمونید؟
How much do I owe?	cheghadr bâyad bedam?	چه قدر باید بدم؟
This is for you.	in barâye shomâst	این برای شماست.
My change, please.	baghiyeye pulam, lotfan	بقیه پولم، لطفاً.

Bus/Subway		اتوبوس / مترو
		otobus / metro
English	**Pronunciation**	**Persian**
Where is the nearest bus stop?	nazdiktarin ishtgâhe otobus kojâst?	نزدیکترین ایستگاه اتوبوس کجاست؟
Where is the nearest subway station?	nazdiktarin istgâhe metro kojâst?	نزدیکترین ایستگاه مترو کجاست؟
Does this bus go there?	in otobus unjâ mire?	این اتوبوس اونجا می ره؟

Bus/Subway		اتوبوس/مترو
		otobus / metro
English	**Pronunciation**	**Persian**
Which bus goes to downtown?	kodum otobus be markaze shahr mire?	کدوم اتوبوس به مرکز شهر می ره؟
Which bus goes to the airport?	kodum otobus be forudgâh mire?	کدوم اتوبوس به فرودگاه می ره؟
What time does the next bus for the airport leave?	otobuse badi barâye forudgâh che sâati harkat mikone?	اتوبوس بعدی برای فرودگاه چه ساعتی حرکت می کنه؟
What time does the last bus for the airport leave?	otobus âkhar barâye forudgâh che sâati harkat mikone?	اتوبوس آخر برای فرودگاه چه ساعتی حرکت می کنه؟
Where do I buy a ticket?	az kojâ mitunim bilit bekharam?	از کجا می تونم بلیط بخرم؟
What's the fare?	kerâye chande?	کرایه چنده؟
How much is the fare to here?	kerâye tâ injâ chande?	کرایه تا اینجا چنده؟
Do I have to pay extra for my baggage?	bâyad barâye vasâyelam mablaghe ezâfi bedam?	باید برای وسایلم مبلغ اضافی بدم؟
Can I buy a monthly pass?	mitunam ye bilite mâhâne bekharam?	می تونم یه بلیط ماهانه بخرم؟
Can I buy a weekly pass?	mitunam ye bilite haftegi bekharam?	می تونم یه بلیط هفتگی بخرم؟
Please tell me where to get off.	lotfan be man begid kojâ piyâde besham	لطفاً به من بگید کجا پیاده بشم

English	Pronunciation	Persian
I would like to get off here, please.	lotfan mano injâ piyâde konid	لطفاً منو اینجا پیاده کنید.
Next stop, please.	istgâhe badi lotfan	ایستگاه بعدی، لطفاً.
I want to cancel this ticket.	mikhâm in bilit ro bâtel konam	می خوام این بلیط رو باطل کنم.
adult	bozorgsâl	بزرگسال
child	kudak	کودک
coach	otobus	اتوبوس
conductor	mas'ule bilit	مسئول بلیط
fare	kerâye	کرایه
ticket	bilit	بلیط
bus stop	istgâhe otobus	ایستگاه اتوبوس
subway map	naghsheye metro	نقشه مترو
schedule	jadvale zamâni	جدول زمانی
transfer/connection	ta'vize vasileye naghliye	تعویض وسیله نقلیه
No entry	vorud mamnu'	ورود ممنوع

Car rental		کرایه ماشین /kerâyeye mâshin/
English	Pronunciation	Persian
I want to rent a car.	man mikhâm ye mâshin kerâye konam	من می خوام یه ماشین کرایه کنم.
I want to rent a motorcycle.	man mikhâm ye motorsiklet kerâye konam	من می خوام یه موتورسیکلت کرایه کنم.

Car rental		كرايه ماشين /kerâyeye mâshin/
English	**Pronunciation**	**Persian**
I want to rent a car with a driver.	man mikhâm ye mâshin bâ rânande kerâye konam	من می خوام یه ماشین با راننده کرایه کنم.
automatic transmission	dande otomât	دنده اتوماتیک
What papers do I need with me?	che madâreki bâyad dâshte bâsham?	چه مدارکی باید داشته باشم؟
This is my international driving permit.	in mojaveze beynolmelaliye rânandegiye mane	این مجوز بین المللی رانندگی منه
What does it cost per day?	kerâyeye ruzâne chand mishe?	کرایه روزانه چند می شه؟
What does it cost per kilometer?	kerâye kilumetri chand mishe?	کرایه کیلومتری چند می شود؟
Does the price include insurance?	in gheimat shâmele bime hast?	این قیمت شامل بیمه هست؟
How long is the minimum rental period?	hadeaghale zamâne kerâye chande?	حداقل زمان کرایه چنده؟
Do I need to pay a deposit?	bâyad vadi'e bedam?	باید ودیعه بدم؟
Does the car have gas?	mâshin benzin dâre?	ماشین بنزین داره؟
What kind of fuel does it take?	che nô' sukhti masraf mikone?	چه نوع سوختی مصرف می کنه؟
I would like to try out the car.	mikhâm mâshin ro emtehân konam	می خوام ماشین رو امتحان کنم.
Where can I return it?	kojâ mitunam un ro bargardunam?	کجا می تونم اون رو

English	Pronunciation	کرایه ماشین /kerâyeye mâshin/ Persian
		بر گردونم؟
Should I return the car with a full tank?	bâyad mâshin ro bâ bâke por bargardunam?	باید ماشین رو با باک پر بر گردونم؟
Please send a car to my hotel.	lotfan ye mâshin be hotele man beferestid	لطفاً یه ماشین به هتل من بفرستید.
car rental office/rent-a-car	daftare kerâyeye mâshin	دفتر کرایه ماشین
rental agreement	tavâfoghnvmeye kerâye	توافق نامه کرایه
tank	bâk	باک
insurance	bime	بیمه

English	Pronunciation	رانندگی -پارک کردن /rânandegi - pârk kardan/ Persian
Where can I park?	kojâ mitunam pârk konam?	کجا می تونم پارک کنم؟
How long can I park here?	che modat mitunam injâ pârk konam?	چه مدت می تونم اینجا پارک کنم؟
Must I pay to park here?	cheghadr bâyad barâye pârk tu injâ bedam?	چقدر باید برای پارک تو اینجا بدم؟
What's the charge per hour?	sâati chande?	ساعتی چنده؟

Driving/Parking		راننده گی -پارک کردن /rânandegi - pârk kardan/
English	**Pronunciation**	**Persian**
What's the charge per day?	ruzâne chande?	روزانه چنده؟
Where is the nearest garage?	nazdiktarin gârâzh kojâst?	نزدیکترین گاراژ کجاست؟
Where is the nearest gas station?	nazdiktarin pompe benzin kojâst?	نزدیکترین پمپ بنزین کجاست؟
Where is the nearest parking lot?	nazdiktarin pârking kojâst?	نزدیکترین پارکینگ کجاست؟
Where is the exit to the highway?	khoruji be bozorgrvh kojâst?	خروجی به بزرگراه کجاست؟
Where does this road go?	in jâde be kojâ mire?	این جاده به کجا می ره؟
Can you show me where I am on the map?	momkene ruye naghshe be man neshun bedid kojâ hastam?	ممکنه روی نقشه به من نشون بدید کجا هستم؟
In which direction should I go?	az kodum taraf bâyad beram?	از کدوم طرف باید برم؟
road	jâde	جاده
construction zone	jâde dar daste ta'mire	جاده در دست تعمیر است
crossroads	chârâh	چهارراه
turn (of the road)	pich	پیچ
traffic lights	cherâghe râhnamâ	چراغ راهنما
road sign	tâbloye râhnamâyi va rânandegi	تابلوی راهنمایی و رانندگی
bicycle path	râhe docharkhe	راه دوچرخه

LearnPersianOnline.com

Driving/Parking		راننده گی -پارک کردن /rânandegi - pârk kardan/
English	**Pronunciation**	**Persian**
dashboard	dâshbord	داشبورد
driver license	govâhinâmeye rânandegi	گواهینامه رانندگی
driver's seat	sandaliye rânande	صندلی راننده
east	shargh	شرق
first	aval	اول
free parking	pârkinge râyegân	پارکینگ رایگان
highway	bozorgrâh	بزرگراه
left	chap	چپ
next	ba'd	بعد
north	shomâl	شمال
parking	pârking	پارکینگ
pedestrian	âbere piyâde	عابر پیاده
pedestrian zone	mantagheye makhsuse âbere piyâde	منطقه مخصوص عابر پیاده
right	râst	راست
south	jonub	جنوب
speed	sor'at	سرعت
speedometer	sor'atsanj	سرعت سنج
straight	mostaghim	مستقیم
toll parking	pârkinge avârezi	پارکینگ عوارضی

Driving/Parking		رانندگی -پارک کردن /rânandegi - pârk kardan/
English	Pronunciation	Persian
toll road	jâdeye avârezi	جاده عوارضی
truck	kâmion	کامیون
tunnel	tunel	تونل
west	gharb	غرب

At the service station		در مرکز سرویس / dar markaze servis/
English	Pronunciation	Persian
antifreeze	zede yakh	ضد یخ
automatic	otomâtik	اتوماتیک
engine	motor	موتور
exhaust	egzoz	اگزوز
license plate	pelâk	پلاک
gasoline	benzin	بنزین
I need unleaded.	man benzine bedune sorb mikhâm	من بنزین بدون سرب می خوام.
I need regular.	man ma'muli mikhâm	من معمولی می خوام.
I need super.	man super mikhâm	من سوپر می خوام.
I need diesel.	man dizel mikhâm	من دیزل می خوام.
Do you do repairs?	ta'mirât anjâm midid?	تعمیرات انجام می دید؟

At the service station		در مرکز سرویس / dar markaze servis/
English	**Pronunciation**	**Persian**
Can you check it for me?	mitunid un ro barâye man chek konid?	می تونید اون رو برای من چک کنید؟
Check the oil, please.	roghan ro lotfan chek konid	روغن رو لطفاً چک کنید.
Check the air in the tires, please.	bâde tâyerhâ ro lotfan chek konid	باد تایرها رو لطفاً چک کنید.
Check the battery, please.	bâtri ro lotfan chek konid	باتری رو لطفاً چک کنید.
Check the brakes, please.	tormozhâ ro lotfan chek konid	ترمزها رو لطفاً چک کنید.
I would like an oil change, please.	man mikhâm roghan ro avaz konid	من می خوام روغن رو تعویض کنید
I need a new battery.	man ye bâtriye no lâzem dâram	من یه باتری نو لازم دارم.
I need new spark plugs.	man sham'hâye no lâzem dâram	من شمع های نو لازم دارم.
I need a new fan belt.	man tasme parvâneye no lâzem dâram	من تسمه پروانه نو لازم دارم.

Out of order		نیاز به تعمیر /niyâz be ta'mir/
English	**Pronunciation**	**Persian**
The engine won't start.	motor roshan nemishe	موتور روشن نمی شه
The engine gets very hot.	motor kheili dâgh mikone	موتور خیلی داغ می کنه.
It's noisy.	kheili saro sedâ mikone	خیلی سر و صدا می کنه.

Out of order		نیاز به تعمیر /niyâz be ta'mir/
English	**Pronunciation**	**Persian**
Something is making a noise.	ye chizi saro sedâ mikone	یه چیزی سر و صدا می کنه.
I have a flat tire.	man panchar kardam	من پنچر کردم.
There is something wrong with the oil pressure.	feshâre roghan moshkel dâre	فشار روغن مشکل داره.
There is something wrong with the electrical system.	sisteme bargh moshkel dâre	سیستم برق مشکل داره.
There is something wrong with the fan belt.	tasme parvâne moshkel dâre	تسمه پروانه مشکل داره.
There is something wrong with the gear shift.	ahrome dande moshkel dâre	اهرم دنده مشکل داره.
There is something wrong with the ignition.	sisteme jaraghe moshkel dâre	سیستم جرقه مشکل داره.
There is something wrong with the starter.	estârt moshkel dâre	استارت مشکل داره.
There is something wrong with the transmission.	ja'be dande moshkel dâre	جعبه دنده مشکل داره.
The headlight doesn't work.	cherâghe jolo kâr nemikone	چراغ جلو کار نمی کنه.
The battery is dead.	bâtri khâli shode	باتری خالی شده
Do you have spare parts?	ghataâte yadaki dârid?	قطعات یدکی دارید؟
We're out of gas.	benzin tamum shode	بنزین تموم شده

LearnPersianOnline.com

I have locked my keys in the car.	man kelidâmo tu mâshin jâ gozâshtam va daro ghofl kardam	من کلیدامو تو ماشین جا گذاشتم و در رو قفل کردم.
The car broke down. Please send someone for it.	mâshin kharâb shod. lotfan ye nafar ro beferestid	ماشین خراب شد. لطفاً یه نفر رو بفرستید.
Can you send a mechanic?	momkene ye mekânik beferestid?	ممکنه یه مکانیک بفرستید؟
Can you send a tow truck?	momkene ye kâmiyone yadakesh beferestid?	ممکنه یه کامیون یدک کش بفرستید؟
Can you repair the car?	mitunid mâshin ro ta'mir konid?	می تونید ماشین رو تعمیر کنید؟
How long will it take to repair the car?	ta'mire mâshin cheghadr tul mikeshe?	تعمیر ماشین چقدر طول می کشه؟
Are the repairs covered by my insurance?	bimeye man hazineye ta'mirât ro pushesh mide?	بیمه من هزینه تعمیرات رو پوشش می ده؟
Will you give me an itemized bill?	momkene ye surathesab mored be mored be man bedid?	ممکنه یه صورتحساب مورد به مورد به من بدید؟
Will you call me when the car is ready?	vaghti mâshin âmâde shod mano khabar mikonid?	وقتی ماشین آماده شد منو خبر می کنید؟
Can you lend me a jack?	momkene ye jak be man gharz bedid?	ممکنه یه جک به من قرض بدید؟
blinker	felâsher	فلاشر
brake pedal	pedâle tormoz	پدال ترمز

brakes	tormoz	ترمز
bumper	separ	سپر
clutch	kelâch	کلاچ
fender	zarbegir	ضربه گیر
gas pedal	pedâle gâz	پدال گاز
gear shift	ahrome dande	اهرم دنده
hand brake	tormoz dasti	ترمز دستی
headlight	cherâghe jolo	چراغ جلو
hood	kâput	کاپوت
ignition	sisteme jaraghe	سیستم جرقه
rearview mirror	âyineye aghab	آینه عقب
seat belt	kamarband	کمربند
side mirror	âyineye baghal	آینه بغل
spare wheel	charkhe zâpâs	چرخ زاپاس
steering wheel	farmân	فرمان
taillight	cherâghe aghab	چراغ عقب
trunk	sandughe aghab	صندوق عقب
turn signal	cherâghe râhnamâ	چراغ راهنما
wheel	charkh	چرخ
windshield	shisheye jolo	شیشه جلو
windshield wiper	barf pâk kon	برف پاک کن

Communication Means

راههای ارتباطی

/râhâye ertebâti/

Old picture of Tehran

English	Pronunciation	اداره پست /edâreye post/ Persian
Post Office		
contents	mohtaviyât	محتویات
envelope	pâkate nâme	پاکت نامه
fragile	shekastani	شکستنی
insured	bime shode	بیمه شده
letter	nâme	نامه
mailbox	sandughe posti	صندوق پستی
mailing address	neshâniye posti	نشانی پستی
package	baste	بسته
postcard	kârte postâl	کارت پستال
registered	sefâreshi	سفارشی
return address	neshâniye bâzgasht	نشانی بازگشت
stamp	tamr	تمبر
to/from	be/az	به/از
zip code	kode posti	کد پستی
Where is the nearest post office?	nazdiktarin edâreye post kojâst?	نزدیکترین اداره پست کجاست؟
Where is the nearest Internet cafe?	nazdiktarin kâfinet kojâst?	نزدیکترین کافی نت کجاست؟
Would you please direct me to the post office?	momkene râhe edâreye post ro be man neshun bedid?	ممکنه راه اداره پست رو به من نشون بدید؟

Where is the general delivery?	sho'beye daryâfte nâme kojâst?	شعبه دریافت نامه کجاست؟
Where is the mailbox?	sandughe posti kojâst?	صندوق پستی کجاست؟
I want to send this by registered mail.	man mikhâm in ro bâ poste sefâreshi beferestam	من می خوام این رو با پست سفارشی بفرستم.
I want to send this by express post.	man mikhâm in ro bâ poste pishtâz beferestam	من می خوام این رو با پست پیشتاز بفرستم.
I want to send this by airmail.	man mikhâm in ro bâ poste havâyi beferestam	من می خوام این رو با پست هوایی بفرستم.
How much do stamps cost for these letters?	tamre in nâmehâ chand mishe?	تمبر این نامه ها چند می شه؟
Do you know what the postage is to USA?	midunid hazineye post tâ orupâ chande?	می دونید هزینه پست تا اروپا چنده؟
Where can I get stamps and postcards?	az kojâ mitunam tamr va kârte postâl begiram?	از کجا می تونم تمبر و کارت پستال بگیرم؟
Can you send it to this address in USA?	momkene in ro be in neshuni tu âmrikâ beferestid?	ممکنه این رو به این نشونی تو آمریکا بفرستید؟
I need a pen.	man ye khodkâr lâzem dâram	من یه خودکار لازم دارم.

Telephone		تلفن
		/telefon/
English	**Pronunciation**	**Persian**
Where can I find a public phone around here?	kojâ mitunam in havâli ye telefone omumi peidâ konam?	کجا می تونم این حوالی یه تلفن عمومی پیدا کنم؟
I would like to make an international call.	man mikhâm ye tamâs beinolmelali begiram	من می خوام یه تماس بین المللی بگیرم.
I would like to make a credit card call.	man mikhâm ye tamâs bâ kârte etebâri begiram	من می خوام یه تماس با کارت اعتباری بگیرم.
How much per minute?	daghigheyi chande?	دقیقه ای چنده؟
The line is busy.	khat eshghâle	خط اشغاله
Can I dial directly?	mitunam mostaghiman shomâre begiram?	می تونم مستقیماً شماره بگیرم؟
May I speak to the manager?	momkene bâ modir sohbat konam?	ممکنه با مدیر صحبت کنم؟
May I use your phone?	momkene az telefone shomâ estefâde konam?	ممکنه از تلفن شما استفاده کنم؟
Can you dial for me?	mitunid barâye man shomâre begirid?	می تونید برای من شماره بگیرید؟
area code	kode mantaghe	کد منطقه
country code	kode keshvar	کد کشور
international assistance	khadamâte beinolmelali	خدمات بین المللی
international call	tamâse beinolmelali	تماس بین المللی
local call	tamâse mahali	تماس محلی

Telephone		تلفن /telefon/
English	**Pronunciation**	**Persian**
operator	operâtor	اپروتور
out of service	kharâb	خراب
telephone card	kârte telefon	کارت تلفن
telephone directory	râhnamâye telefon	راهنمای تلفن
toll-free call	telefone râyegân	تلفن رایگان
Can you talk for me?	mitunid barâye man sohbat konid?	می تونید برای من صحبت کنید؟
Hold the line, please.	lotfan poshte khat bemunid	لطفاً پشت خط بمونید.
I will call again later.	man dobâre zang mizanam	من دوباره زنگ می زنم.
May I ask who's calling?	mitunam beporsam esme shomâ chiye?	می تونم بپرسم اسم شما چیه؟
How do you spell that?	momkene un ro heji konid?	ممکنه اون رو هجی کنید؟
I got the wrong number.	man shomâraro eshtebâh gereftam	من شماره رو اشتباه گرفتم.
Please ask him to call me.	lotfan azash bekhâyn bâ man tamâs begire	لطفاً ازش بخواین با من تماس بگیره
Can I leave a message?	momkene peighâm bezâram?	ممکنه پیغام بذارم؟
What time is he expected back?	che moghe barmigarde?	چه موقع بر می گرده؟
Thank you for calling.	az tamâse shomâ mamnunam	از تماس شما ممنونم

	Internet	
English	**Pronunciation**	**Pronunciation**
I want to send a message by e-mail.	man mikhâm ye peyghâm bâ imeil befereftam	من می خوام یه پیغام با ایمیل بفرستم.
I want to send a message by fax.	man mikhâm ye peighâm bâ faks beferestam	من می خوام یه پیغام با فکس بفرستم.
What's your e-mail address?	imeile shomâ chiye?	ایمیل شما چیه؟
What are the charges per hour for internt?	hazineye internet sâati chande?	هزینه اینترنت ساعتی چنده؟
How do I log on?	chetor mitunam vâred besham?	چطور می تونم وارد بشم؟

Eating

خوردنی ها
/khordanihâ/

Fruits/Vegetables		میوه ها/سبزیجات /mivehâ – sabzijât/
English	**Pronunciation**	**Persian**
apples	sib	سیب
apricots	zardâlu	زردآلو
asparagus	mârchube	مارچوبه
avocado	âvokâdo	آوکادو
bananas	môz	موز
beans	lubiyâ	لوبیا
blueberries	zoghâl akhte	زغال اخته
broccoli	kalame berokli	کلم بروکلی
cabbage	kalam	کلم
carrots	havij	هویج
cauliflower	gole kalam	گل کلم
celery	karafs	کرفس
cherries	gilâs	گیلاس
corn	zorat	ذرت
cucumbers	khiyâr	خیار
eggplant	bâdemjun	بادمجان
figs	anjir	انجیر
grapefruit	grip frut	گریپ فروت
grapes	angur	انگور
green beans	lubiyâ sabz	لوبیا سبز

Fruits/Vegetables		میوه ها/سبزیجات /mivehâ – sabzijât/
English	**Pronunciation**	**Persian**
kale	kalampich	کلم پیچ
kiwi	kivi	کیوی
lemons	limu	لیمو
lettuce	kâhu	کاهو
lime	limu torsh	لیمو ترش
mangos	anbe	انبه
melons	kharboze	خربزه
mushrooms	ghârch	قارچ
olives	zeitun	زیتون
onions	piyâz	پیاز
oranges	porteghâl	پرتقال
peaches	holu	هلو
pears	golâbi	گلابی
peas	nokhod farangi	نخود فرنگی
pickles	khiyâr shur	خیار شور
plums	âlu	آلو
potato	sibzamini	سیب زمینی
pumpkin	kadu tanbal	کدو تنبل
radishes	torobche	تربچه
raisins	keshmesh	کشمش

Fruits/Vegetables		میوه ها/سبزیجات /mivehâ – sabzijât/
English	**Pronunciation**	**Persian**
raspberries	tameshk	تمشک
red beans	lubiyâ ghermez	لوبیا قرمز
rhubarb	rivâs	ریواس
spinach	esfenâj	اسفناج
strawberries	tut farangi	توت فرنگی
tangerines	nârangi	نارنگی
tomatoes	goje farangi	گوجه فرنگی
vegetables	sabzijât	سبزیجات
watermelons	hendevâne	هندوانه
zucchini	kadu	کدو

Spices		ادویه جات /adviyejât/
English	**Pronunciation**	**Persian**
basil	reyhân	ریحان
caraway/cumin	zire	زیره
cardamom	hel	هل
cayenne pepper	felfele hendi	فلفل هندی
chamomile	bâbune	بابونه
chili	felfele ghermez	فلفل قرمز

Spices		ادویه جات /adviyejât/
English	**Pronunciation**	**Persian**
cinnamon	dârchin	دارچین
cloves	mikhake khoshk shode	میخک خشک شده
coriander	geshniz	گشنیز
dill	shevid	شوید
garlic	sir	سیر
ginger	zanjabil	زنجبیل
oregano	âvishan	آویشن
parsley	ja'fari	جعفری
pepper	felfel	فلفل
saffron	za'ferun	زعفرون
sesame	konjed	کنجد
spearmint	na'nâye tond	نعنای تند
thyme	âvishan	آویشن
turmeric	zardchube	زردچوبه

Seafood		غذاهای دریایی /ghazâhâye daryâyi
English	**Pronunciation**	**Persian**
catfish	gorbe mâhi	گربه ماهی
caviar	khâviyâr	خاویار
clams	halezun	حلزون
cod	mâhi roghan	ماهی روغن

Seafood		غذاهای دریایی /ghazâhâye daryâyi
English	**Pronunciation**	**Persian**
fish	mâhi	ماهی
herring	shâh mâhi	شاه ماهی
lobster , crab , crayfish	kharchang	خرچنگ
octopus	okhtâpus	اختاپوس
oyster	sadaf	صدف
perch	mâhi khârdâr	ماهی خاردار
pike	ordak mâhi	اردک ماهی
red snapper	mâhi sorkhu	ماهی سرخو
salmon	mâhi âzâd	ماهی آزاد
shrimp/prawn	meygu	میگو
squid	mâhi morakab	ماهی مرکب
trout	mâhi ghezel âlâ	ماهی قزل آلا
tuna	mâhiye ton	ماهی تن
whitefish	mâhi sefid	ماهی سفید

Meat		گوشت /gusht/
English	**Pronunciation**	**Persian**
beef	gushte gâv	گوشت گاو
chicken	juje	جوجه
duck	ordak	اردک

Meat		گوشت /gusht/
English	**Pronunciation**	**Persian**
lamb	gushte bare	گوشت بره
minced meat	gushte charkh karde	گوشت چرخ کرده
pork	gushte khuk	گوشت خوک
poultry	morgh	مرغ
rabbit	khargush	خرگوش
schnitzel	shensil	شنیسل
steak	esteyk	استیک
turkey	bughalamun	بوقلمون
veal	gushte gusâle	گوشت گوساله

Grocery		خواربار /khâro bâr/
English	**Pronunciation**	**Persian**
almonds	bâdâm	بادام
bread	nân	نان
bun	nâne komâj	نان کماج
candy	âbnabât	آبنبات
cereals	bereshtuk	برشتوک
cheese	panir	پنیر
chestnuts	shâhbalut	شاه بلوط
chocolate	shokolât	شکلات
coconut	nârgil	نارگیل

	Grocery	خواربار /khâro bâr/
English	**Pronunciation**	**Persian**
cream	khâme	خامه
cream cheese	panire khâme'i	پنیر خامه ای
dressing	sos	سس
eggs	tokhmemorgh	تخم مرغ
hazelnut/filberts	fandogh	فندق
ice cream	bastani	بستنی
ketchup	sose kachâb	سس کچاپ
mayonnaise	mâyonez	مایونز
milk	shir	شیر
mustard	khardal	خردل
nuts	âjil	آجیل
oat bread	nâne jô	نان جو
olive oil	roghan zeytun	روغن زیتون
peanuts	bâdâm zamini	بادام زمینی
pistachios	peste	پسته
pumpernickel bread	nâne siyâh	نان سیاه
roll	nâne gerd	نان گرده
sausage	sosis	سوسیس
vinegar	serke	سرکه
walnuts	gerdu	گردو

Grocery		خواربار /khâro bâr/
English	**Pronunciation**	**Persian**
white bread	nâne sefid	نان سفید
whole wheat bread	nâne sefide kâmel	نان سفید کامل
yogurt	mâste mive'i	ماست میوه ای

Drinks		نوشیدنی ها /nushidanihâ
English	**Pronunciation**	**Persian**
Alcohol	alekol	الکل
alcohol-free	bedune alekol	بدون الکل
beer	âbjo	آبجو
cappuccino	kâpâchino	کاپاچینو
cocktail	koktel	کوکتل
cocoa	shir kâkâu	شیر کاکائو
coffee	ghahve	قهوه
draft beer	âbjoye boshke'i	آبجوی بشکه ای
green tea	chây sabz	چای سبز
hot chocolate	shokolâte dâgh	شکلات داغ
iced tea	âisti	آیس تی
juice	âbmive	آبمیوه
lemonade	limunâd	لیموناد
long drink	nushidaniye bozorg	نوشیدنی بزرگ

Drinks		نوشیدنی ها /nushidanihâ
English	**Pronunciation**	**Persian**
mineral water	âb ma'dani	آب معدنی
orange juice	âbporteghâl	آب پرتقال
red wine	sharâbe ghermez	شراب قرمز
shot	gilâs	گیلاس
sparkling wine	shâmpân	شامپاین
tea	chây	چای
tonic	tonik	تونیک
white wine	sharâbe sefid	شراب سفید
wine	sharâb	شراب
with cinnamon	bâ dârchin	با دارچین
with cream	bâ khâme	با خامه
with ice	bâ yakh	با یخ
with lemon	bâ limu	با لیمو
with sugar	bâ shekar	با شکر

At the restaurant		در رستوران / dar resturân /
English	**Pronunciation**	**Persian**
apple pie	pâye sib	پای سیب
baked	pokhte	پخته
barbecued	kabâbi	کبابی

At the restaurant		در رستوران / dar resturân /
English	**Pronunciation**	**Persian**
bean soup	supe lubiyâ	سوپ لوبیا
beef stew	tâskabâbe gâv	تاس کباب گاو
beef stroganoff	bifestrâgânof	بیف استراگانف
bitter	talkh	تلخ
boiled	âbpaz	آب پز
boiled beef	gushte gave âb paz	گوشت گاو آب پز
brisket	gushte sine	گوشت سینه
cake	keik	کیک
cheeseburger	chizberger	چیزبرگر
chicken breast	sineye morgh	سینه مرغ
chicken wings	bâle juje	بال جوجه
chop	gushte bâ ostekhân	گوشت با استخوان
coleslaw	sâlâde kalam	سالاد کلم
cookies	biskuyit	بیسکویت
cornflakes	bereshtuk	برشتوک
cutlet	kabâb	کباب
dessert	deser	دسر
filet	file	فیله
flan	keike mive'i	کیک میوه
fresh	tâze	تازه

At the restaurant		در رستوران / dar resturân /
English	**Pronunciation**	**Persian**
fruit salad	sâlâde mive	سالاد میوه
Greek salad	sâlâde unâni	سالاد یونانی
Green salad	sâlâde sabzijât	سالاد سبزیجات
green salad	sâlâde sabzijât	سالاد سبزیجات
hamburger	hamberger	همبرگر
hard-boiled eggs	tokhmemoreghe seft	تخم مرغ سفت
homemade	khânegi	خانگی
hot dog	hâtdâg	هات داگ
jam	morabâ	مربا
kebab	kâbâb	کباب
kidneys	gholve	قلوه
lamb stew	tâskabâbe bare	تاس کباب بره
loin	goshte gorde	گوشت گرده
macaroni	mâkâroni	ماکارونی
main course	ghazâye asli	غذای اصلی
mashed	leh shode	له شده
medium	nimpaz	نیم پز
minced	khord karde	خرد کرده
mushroom soup	supe ghârch	سوپ قارچ
noodles	reshteye farangi	رشته فرنگی

At the restaurant		در رستوران / dar resturân /
English	**Pronunciation**	**Persian**
omelet	omlet	املت
onion soup	supe piyâz	سوپ پیاز
pancake	pankeyk	پنکیک
pasta	pâstâ	پاستا
pizza	pitzâ	پیتزا
poached	âbpaz shode	آب پز شده
pot roast	ghorme	قورمه
potato chips	chips	چیپس
potato salad	sâlâde sibzamini	سالاد سیب زمینی
pudding	puding	پودینگ
purée	pure	پوره
rare	khâm	خام
ribs	dande	دنده
rice	berenj	برنج
ripe	reside	رسیده
roast chicken	juje kabâb	جوجه کباب
roasted	kabâbi	کبابی
salad	sâlâd	سالاد
salty	shur	شور
sandwich	sândevich	ساندویچ

At the restaurant		در رستوران / dar resturân /
English	**Pronunciation**	**Persian**
smoked	dudi	دودی
soft-boiled eggs	tokhmemorghe asali	تخم مرغ عسلی
sour	torsh	ترش
spaghetti	espâgeti	اسپاگتی
spicy/hot	tond	تند
stewed	khoreshi	خورشتی
stuffed	por shode	پر شده
sweet	shirin	شیرین
tastless	bi maze	بی مزه
tasty	khoshmaze	خوشمزه
tender	narm	نرم
toast	nâne tost	نان تست
tongue	zabân	زبان
topping	châshniye ruye ghazâ	چاشنی روی غذا
turkey breast	sineye bughalamun	سینه بوقلمون
vanilla	vânil	وانیل

Finance		مال – پول /mâl - pul/
English	**Pronunciation**	**Persian**
Where is the nearest currency exchange office?	nazdiktarin sarâfi kojâst?	نزدیکترین صرافی کجاست؟
How late is the bank open?	bânk tâ key bâze?	بانک تا کی بازه؟
How late is the exchange point open?	sarâfi tâ key bâze?	صرافی تا کی بازه؟
ATM (Automated Teller Machine)	dastgâhe khodpardâz	دستگاه خودپرداز
I would like to open a savings account.	man mikhâm ye hesâbe pasandâz bâz konam	من می خوام یه حساب پس انداز باز کنم.
I would like to open a checking account.	man mikhâm ye hesâbe jâri bâz konam	من می خوام یه حساب جاری باز کنم.
I would like to deposit some money.	man mikhâm meghdâri pul vâriz konam	من می خوام مقداری پول واریز کنم.
I would like to withdraw some money.	man mikhâm meghdâri pul bardâsht konam	من می خوام مقداری پول برداشت کنم.
I need a withdrawal slip.	man ye ghabze bardâsht mikhâm	من یه قبض برداشت می خوام.
I need a deposit slip.	man ye ghabze vâriz mikhâm	من یه قبض واریز می خوام.
Where do I sign?	kojâ ro bâyad emzâ konam?	کجا رو باید امضاء کنم؟
bills	eskenâs	اسکناس

Finance		مال – پول /mâl - pul/
English	**Pronunciation**	**Persian**
cash	pule naghd	پول نقد
coins	seke	سکه
commission	haghe komisiyon	حق کمیسیون
Deposit/Withdrawal	vâriz/bardâsht	واریز/برداشت
interest rate	nerkhe bahre	نرخ بهره
MasterCard	master kârt	مستر کارت
money	pul	پول
receipt	resid	رسید
traveler's check	cheke mosâferati	چک مسافرتی
Visa	vizâ	ویزا
I would like to open an account.	man mikhâm ye hesâb bâz konam	من می خوام یه حساب باز کنم.
Is my passport necessary?	gozarnâmeye man lâzeme?	گذرنامه من لازمه؟
This is my identification.	in kârte shenâsayiye mane	این کارت شناسایی منه
Where are the cash machines?	dastgâhe khodpardâz kojâ hastand?	دستگاه های خودپرداز کجا هستند؟
Can I withdraw money on my credit card here?	mitunam az kârte etebârim injâ bardâsht konam?	می تونم از کارت اعتباریم اینجا برداشت کنم؟
Put it on my card.	be kârte man vâriz konid	به کارت من واریز کنید.
Currency Exchange	sarâfi	صرافی

Finance		مال – پول /mâl - pul/
English	Pronunciation	Persian
We buy/sell	mâ mikharim / miforushim	ما می خریم/ می فروشیم
dinar	dinâr	دینار
dollar	dolâr	دلار
euro	yoro	یورو
peso	pezo	پزو
pound	pond	پوند
ruble	rubl	روبل
rupee	rupiye	روپیه
yen	yen	ین
yuan	yuân	یواون
Where can I change money?	kojâ mitunam azr mobâdele konam?	کجا می تونم ارز مبادله کنم؟
What is the exchange rate for euros?	nerkhe mobâdele barâye yoro chande?	نرخ مبادله برای یورو چنده؟
I would like to cash this traveler's check.	man mikhâm in chek mosâferati ro naghd konam	من می خوام این چک مسافرتی رو نقد کنم.
What is the commission?	haghe komisiyon chande?	حق کمیسیون چنده؟
Could you give me change for this bill?	momkene in eskenâs ro barâye man khord konid?	ممکنه این اسکناس رو برای من خرد کنید؟

Shopping		خرید /kharid/
English	**Pronunciation**	**Persian**
Where is the shopping area?	mantagheye kharid kojâst?	منطقه خرید کجاست؟
Where is the nearest bookstore?	nazdiktarin ketâb forushi kojâst?	نزدیکترین کتاب فروشی کجاست؟
Where is the nearest ATM?	nazdiktarin ATM kojâst?	نزدیکترین ای تی ام کجاست؟
Where is the nearest shoe store?	nazdiktarin maghâzeye kafsh forushi kojâst?	نزدیکترن مغازه کفش فروشی کجاست؟
Where is the nearest clothing store?	nazdiktarin forushgâhe pushâk kojast?	نزدیکترین فروشگاه پوشاک کجاست؟
Where is the nearest market?	nazdiktarin bâzâr kojâst?	نزدیکترین بازار کجاست؟
Where is the nearest drugstore?	nazdiktarin dârukhâne kojâst?	نزدیکترین داروخانه کجاست؟
antique store	maghâzeye atighe forushi	مغازه عتیقه فروشی
bookstore	ketâb forushi	کتاب فروشی
camera store	forushgâhe durbin	فروشگاه دوربین
Cash desk	sandugh	صندوق
children's wear	lebâse kudakân	لباس کودکان
clearance sale , sale	harâj	حراج
clothing store	forushgâhe pushâk	فروشگاه پوشاک
Customer service	khadamâte moshtari	خدمات مشتری

Shopping		خرید /kharid/
English	Pronunciation	Persian
department store	forushgâhe bozorg	فروشگاه بزرگ
drugstore	dârukhâne	داروخانه
jewelry store	javâher forushi	جواهر فروشی
knitwear	lebâse bâftani	لباس بافتنی
ladieswear	lebâse zanâne	لباس زنانه
lingerie	lebâse zire zanâne	لباس زیر زنانه
mall/shopping center	markaze kharid	مرکز خرید
market	bâzâr	بازار
menswear	lebâse mardâne	لباس مردانه
minimarket	maghâze	مغازه
newsstand	dakeye ruznâme forushi	دکه روزنامه فروشی
shoe store	kafsh forushi	کفش فروشی
sleepwear	lebâse khâb	لباس خواب
souvenir shop	maghâzeye soghât forushi	مغازه کادو فروشی/سوغات فروشی
sporting goods store	forushgâhe lavâzeme varzeshi	فروشگاه لوازم ورزشی
supermarket	supermârket	سوپرمارکت
toy store	forushgâhe asbâb bâzi	فروشگاه اسباب بازی
Pay here	injâ bepardâzid	اینجا بپردازید
gift	kâdo	کادو

Shopping		خرید /kharid/
English	**Pronunciation**	**Persian**
Service	servis	سرویس
May I pick it up?	momkene un ro bardâram?	ممکنه اون رو بردارم؟
Clothes	lebâs	لباس
I would like to try it on.	mikhâm in ro poro konam	می خوام این رو پرو کنم.
Where's the fitting room?	otâghe poro kojâst?	اتاق پرو کجاست؟
It's too short.	kheili kutâhe	خیلی کوتاهه
It's too long.	kheili bolande	خیلی بلنده
It's too tight.	kheili tange	خیلی تنگه
It's too loose.	kheili goshâde	خیلی گشاده

Clothing		پوشاک / pushâk/
English	**Pronunciation**	**Persian**
I would like to try it on.	mikhâm in ro poro konam	می خوام این رو پرو کنم.
I would like a business suit.	man ye dast koto shalvâre makhsuse kâr mikhâm	من یه دست کت و شلوار مخصوص کار می خوام.
I would like a dress suit.	man ye dast koto shalvâre shab mikhâm	من یه دست کت و شلوار شب می خوام.
Where's the fitting room?	otâghe poro kojâst?	اتاق پرو کجاست؟

It doesn't quite fit me.	kâmelan andâzeye man nist	.کاملاً اندازه من نیست
It's too short.	kheili kutâhe	خیلی کوتاهه
It's too long.	kheili bolande	خیلی بلنده
It's too tight.	kheili tange	خیلی تنگه
It's too loose.	kheili goshâde	خیلی گشاده
tailor-made	dukhte sefâreshi	دوخت سفارشی
bikini	bikini	بیکینی
blouse	boluz	بلوز
boxer shorts	shorte bachedâr	شورت پاچه دار
bra	sutiyan	سوتین
briefs	shorte mardâne	شورت مردانه
coat	kot	کت
cotton	nakh	نخ
fabric	pârche	پارچه
handmade	dast duz	دست دوز
hat	kolâh	کلاه
jacket	kot	کت
jeans	shalvâre jin	شلوار جین
linen	katân	کتان
nylon	nâylon	نایلون
pants	shalvâr	شلوار
pullover	poliver	پلیور

raincoat	bâruni	بارونی
shirt	pirhan	پیرهن
silk	abrisham	ابریشم
skirt	dâman	دامن
socks	jurâb	جوراب
swimming trunks	mâyoye mardâne	مایوی مردانه
swimsuit	mâyoye shenâ	مایوی شنا
T-shirt	tishert	تی شرت
underpants	zirshalvâri	زیرشلواری
underwear	zirpush	زیرپوش
vest	jalighe	جلیقه
wool	pashm	پشم
large (L)	bozorg	بزرگ
small (S)	kuchik	کوچیک
medium (M)	motevaset	متوسط
extra large (XL)	kheili bozorg	خیلی بزرگ
long sleeve	âstin boland	آستین بلند
short sleeve	âstin kutâh	آستین کوتاه

Accessories		لوازم تزئینی
		/ lavâzeme taz'ini /
English	Pronunciation	Persian
Could you show me a selection of silk ties?	momkene kerâvâtâtuno be man neshun bedid?	ممکنه کراواتاتون رو به من نشون بدید؟
Please show me a tie in a solid color.	lotfan ye kerâvâte sâde be man neshun bedid	لطفاً یه کراوات ساده به من نشون دهید.
I would like a pair of sunglasses.	man ye eynake âftâbi mikhâm	من یه عینک آفتابی می خوام.
These glasses are too weak for me.	in eynak barâye man kheili za'ife	این عینک برای من خیلی ضعیفه
backpack	kuleposhti	کوله پشتی
bag	kif	کیف
belt	kamarband	کمربند
eyeglasses	eynak	عینک
genuine leather	charme asl	چرم اصل
gloves	dastkesh	دستکش
handbag	kif dasti	کیف دستی
hard leather	charme khoshk	چرم خشک
imitation leather	charme masnu'i	چرم مصنوعی
scarf	shâl gardan	شال گردن
tie	kerâvât	کراوات
umbrella	chatr	چتر
wallet	kife pul	کیف پول

Accessories		لوازم تزئینی / lavâzeme taz'ini /
English	**Pronunciation**	**Persian**
What material is it made of?	jensesh az chiyc?	جنسش از چیه؟

Electronics		وسایل الکترونیکی / vasâyele elektriki/
English	**Pronunciation**	**Persian**
battery	bâtri	باتری
CD bags	kife sidi	کیف سی دی
cellular phone	mubâyl	موبایل
compact disc (CD)	sidi	سی دی
computer	kâmpiyuter	کامپیوتر
digital	dijitâl	دیجیتال
electric shaver	rishtarâshe barghi	ریش تراش برقی
flash card	felashkârt	فلاش کارت
hairdryer	seshvâr	سشوار
memory stick	kârte hâfeze	کارت حافظه
memory stick	kârte hâfeze	کارت حافظه
mouse	môs	موس
I want to buy a battery.	man mikhâm ye bâtri bekharam	من می خوام یه باتری بخرم.
Have you got any flashlight batteries?	bâtriye cherâgh ghove dârid?	باتری چراغ قوه دارید؟
Have you got any hearing aid batteries?	bâtriye sam'ak dârid?	باتری سمعک دارید؟

Electronics		وسایل الکترونیکی / vasâyele elektriki/
English	Pronunciation	Persian
I would like to have a couple bulbs	man chand tâ lâmp mikhâm	من چند تا لامپ می خوام.
Will you show me how to operate it?	momkene be man begid chetor kâr mikone?	ممکنه به من بگید چطور کار می کنه؟
Is there a guarantee?	gârânti dâre?	گارانتی داره؟
Does it come with instructions?	daftarcheye râhnamâ dâre?	دفترچه راهنما داره؟
I'm looking for a disposable camera.	man donbâle ye durbine yekbâr masraf migardam	من دنبال یه دوربین یکبار مصرف می گردم.
I would like a battery.	man ye bâtri mikhâm	من یه باتری می خوام.

Jewelry		جواهرآلات / javâherâlât/
English	Pronunciation	Persian
I'm looking for a small piece of jewelry.	man donbâle ye ghat'e javâhere kuchik migardam	من دنبال یه قطعه جواهر کوچک می گردم.
I would like a ring.	man ye angoshtar mikhâm	من یه انگشتر می خوام.
bracelet	dastband	دست بند
brooch	sanjâghe sine	سنجاق سینه
chain	zanjir	زنجیر
clock	sâat	ساعت
earrings	gushvâre	گوشواره

Jewelry		جواهرآلات / javâherâlât/
English	**Pronunciation**	**Persian**
gold ring	angoshtare talâ	انگشتر طلا
necklace	gardanband	گردن بند
pendant	âviz	آویز
watch	sâate mochi	ساعت مچی
wedding ring	halgheye ezdevâj	حلقه ازدواج
Have you got any gold earrings?	gushvâreye talâ dârid?	گوشواره طلا دارید؟
Is it handmade?	dast sâze?	دست سازه؟
Is this gold?	talâst?	طلاست؟
Is there a certificate for it?	sanade rasmi dâre?	سند رسمی داره؟
The winder is broken.	dokmeye tanzim kharâb shode	دکمه تنظیم خراب شده
Could you please change the battery in my watch?	momkene bâtriye sâatamo avaz konid?	ممکنه لطفاً باتری ساعتم رو عوض کنید؟
diamond	almâs	الماس
emerald	zomorod	زمرد
gold	talâ	طلا
imitation jewelry	javâhere badali	جواهر بدلی
pearl	morvârid	مروارید
platinum	pelâtin	پلاتین
ruby	yâghute sorkh	یاقوت سرخ
silver	noghre	نقره

English	Pronunciation	Persian ابزارها /abzârhâ/
	gheichi	قیچی
adjustable wrench	âchâr farânse	آچار فرانسه
awl	surâkh kon	سوراخ کن
ax	tabar	تبر
bolt	pich	پیچ
chain	zanjir	زنجیر
chisel	eskene	اسکنه
drill	mate	مته
electrical tape	chasbe bargh	چسب برق
file	sohân	سوهان
funnel	ghif	قیف
hammer	chakosh	چکش
handsaw	are dasti	اره دستی
level	tarâz	تراز
nail	mikh	میخ
nut	vâsher	واشر
Phillips screw driver	pichgushti chârsu	پیچ گوشتی چهارسو
pipe wrench	âchâr lule	آچار لوله
pliers	anbordast	انبردست
plunger	piston	پیستون

Jewelry		جواهرآلات / javâherâlât/
English	**Pronunciation**	**Persian**
rake	changak	چنگک
sandpaper	sombâde	سمباده
scraper	kharâshande	خراشنده
screw driver	pichgushti	پیچ گوشتی
shovel	bil	بیل
stapler	dastgâhe mangene	دستگاه منگنه
tape measure	navâre metr	نوارمتر
tongs	anbor	انبر
toolbox	ja'beye abzâr	جعبه ابزار
wire	sim	سیم
wire stripper	sim lokht kon	سیم لخت کن
wrench	âchâr	آچار

In the Office		در اداره /dar edâre/
English	**Pronunciation**	**Persian**
Calculator	mâshine hesâb	ماشین حساب
Chair	sandal	صندلی
Computer	kâmpiyuter	کامپیوتر
Desk	miz	میز
Diary	daftare yâdâsht	دفتر یادداشت

In the Office		در اداره /dar edâre/
English	**Pronunciation**	**Persian**
Drawer	kesho	کشو
Envelope	pâkate nâme	پاکت نامه
Eraser (= rubber)	pâkon	پاک کن
Filing Cabinet	cabinet	کابینت
Hole-punch	surâkhkon	سوراخ کن
insurance	bime	بیمه
letter	nâme	نامه
mail	post	پست
Paper	kâghaz	کاغذ
Paper clips	kelipse kâghaz	کلیپس کاغذ
Pen	khodkâr	خودکار
Pencil	medâd	مداد
Pencil sharpener	tarâsh	تراش
photocopier	fotokopi	فوتوکپی
post card	kârteposti	کارت پستی
post office box	sandoghe posti	صندق پستی
Report	gozâresh	گزارش
Ruler	khatkesh	خط کش
Scanner	eskâner	اسکنر
Scissors	gheichi	قیچی

In the Office		در اداره /dar edâre/
English	**Pronunciation**	**Persian**
stamp	tambr	تمبر
Stapler	mangane	منگنه
Tape (dispenser)	navâre kâset	نوار کاست
Telephone	telefon	تلفن
zip code	kodeposti	کد پستی

Sightseeing

جاهای دیدنی
/jâhâye didani/

Anahita Mosque

English	Pronunciation	اطلاعات جهانگردان /etelâate jaâhangardân/ Tourist information
Is there a city tour here?	injâ ture shahr hast?	اینجا تور شهر هست؟
I want to go sightseeing.	man mikhâm az jâhâye didani bâzdid konam	من می خوام از جاهای دیدنی بازدید کنم.
What are the main points of interest?	jâhâye didaniye asli kojâ hastand?	جاهای دیدنی اصلی کجا هستند؟
Can you recommend a guide?	mitunid ye râhnamâ moarefi konid?	می تونید یه راهنما معرفی کنید؟
Would you please arrange the trip for me?	momkene safar ro barâye man tartib bedid?	ممکنه سفر رو برای من ترتیب بدید؟
Is it too far to walk?	barâye piyâde raftan kheili dure?	برای پیاده رفتن خیلی دوره؟
Would you please tell me what museums there are here?	momkene lotfan be man begid che muzehâyi injâ hast?	ممکنه لطفاً به من بگید چه موزه هایی اینجا هست؟
Would you please tell me what theaters there are here?	momkene lotfan be man begid che teâtrhâyi injâ hast?	ممکنه لطفاً به من بگویید چه تئاترهایی اینجا هست؟
What time does it start?	che sâati shoru mishe?	چه ساعتی شروع می شه؟
What time do we get back?	che sâati bar migardim?	چه ساعتی بر می گردیم؟
When and where can we meet?	key va kojâ mitunim hamdigaro bebinim?	کی و کجا می تونیم همدیگرو ببینیم؟

		اطلاعات جهانگردان
Tourist information		/etelâate jaâhangardân/

English	Pronunciation	Persian
What sights are we going to see?	che mahalhâyi ro mibinim?	چه محلهایی رو می بینیم؟
Where can I buy a map of the town?	az kojâ mitunam ye naghsheye shahr bekharam?	از کجا می تونم یه نقشه شهر بخرم؟
Is there a theater in this town?	tu in shahr teâtr hast?	تو این شهر تئاتر هست؟
May I use your bathroom?	momkene az dastshuyiye shomâ estefâde konam?	ممکنه از دستشویی شما استفاده کنم؟
Asking the way	porsidane râh	پرسیدن راه
Excuse me. How can I get to this place?	bebakhshid chetor mitunam be in mahal beram?	ببخشید چطور می تونم به این محل برم؟
Where is the church?	kelisâ kojâst?	کلیسا کجاست؟
Where is the art gallery?	negârkhâneye honari kojâst?	نگارخانه هنری کجاست؟
Where is the town hall?	shahrdâri kojâst?	شهرداری کجاست؟
Where is the museum?	muze kojâst?	موزه کجاست؟
Where is the theater?	teâtr kojâst?	تئاتر کجاست؟
Would you tell me how to get to this hotel?	momkene be man begid chetor be in hotel beram?	ممکنه به من بگید چطور به این هتل برم؟
Where is the nearest subway station?	nazdiktarin istgâhe metro kojâst?	نزدیکترین ایستگاه مترو کجاست؟

LearnPersianOnline.com

Tourist information	اطلاعات جهانگردان /etelâate jaâhangardân/

English	Pronunciation	Persian
Where is the nearest taxi stand?	nazdiktarin istgâhe tâksi kojâst?	نزدیکترین ایستگاه تاکسی کجاست؟
Could you please you show me the way to the police station?	momkene râhe istgâhe edâreye polis ro be man neshun bedid?	ممکنه راه اداره پلیس رو به من نشون بدید؟
Could you please show me the way to the hotel?	momkene râhe hotel ro be man neshun bedid?	ممکنه راه هتل رو به من نشون بدید؟
Could you please show me the way to the beach?	momkene râhe sâhel ro be man neshun bedid?	ممکنه راه ساحل رو به من نشون بدید؟
Could you please show me the way to the town center?	momkene râhe markaze shahr ro be man neshun bedid?	ممکنه راه مرکز شهر رو به من نشون بدید؟
Which way is downtown?	markaze shahr az kodum tarafe?	مرکز شهر از کدوم طرفه؟
Please draw a map here.	lotfan ye naghshe injâ bekeshid	لطفاً یه نقشه اینجا بکشید.
Where are we now?	hâlâ kojâ hastim?	حالا کجا هستیم؟
What is the name of this street?	esme in khiyâbun chiye?	اسم این خیابون چیه؟
What is the name of this district?	esme in nâhiye chiye?	اسم این ناحیه چیه؟
What is the name of this town?	esme in shahr chiye?	اسم این شهر چیه؟
Is it far from here?	ia injâ kheili dure?	از اینجا خیلی دوره؟

English	Pronunciation	سرگرمی/سینما/تئاتر / sargarmi / sinamâ / teâtr /
Entertainment/Movies/Theater		

English	Pronunciation	Persian
Do you have a program of events?	barnâmeye ruydâdhâ ro dârid?	برنامه رویدادها رو دارید؟
Could you recommend a concert?	momkene ye konsert be man tosiye konid?	ممکنه یه کنسرت به من توصیه کنید؟
Would you like to go to the theater with me?	dust dârid bâ man be teâtr biyâyid?	دوست دارید با من به تئاتر بیایید؟
Are there any seats left for tonight?	jâyi barâye emshab khâli munde?	جایی برای امشب خالی مونده؟
What time does the concert start?	konsert che sâati shoru mishe?	کنسرت چه ساعتی شروع می شه؟
How long will it run?	che modat tul mikeshe?	چه مدت طول می کشه؟
I will get the tickets.	man bilit migiram	من بلیط می گیرم.
Could I have the program, please?	momkene barnâme ro be man bedid?	ممکنه برنامه رو به من بدید؟
Entertainment/Nightlife	sargarmi/tafrihâte shabâne	سرگرمی/تفریحات شبانه
Is it far to the party place?	ta mahale mehmâni kheili râhe?	تا محل مهمانی خیلی راهه؟
Is it far to the bowling club?	tâ bâshgâhe buling kheili râhe?	تا باشگاه بولینگ خیلی راهه؟
What type of music do they play?	che nô' musighi mizane?	چه نوع موسیقی می زنه؟
Is there a cover charge?	vorudi dâre?	ورودی داره؟

At the museum		در موزه /dar muze/
English	**Pronunciation**	**Persian**
Is the museum open to the public?	moze barâye bâzdide omum bâze?	موزه برای بازدید عموم بازه؟
What time does the museum open?	muze che sâati bâz mishe?	موزه چه ساعتی باز می شه؟
What time does the museum close?	muze che sâati ta'til mishe?	موزه چه ساعتی تعطیل می شه؟
Is there access for the disabled?	barâye afrâde ma'lul emkâne dastresi vojud dâre?	برای افراد معلول امکان دسترسی وجود داره؟
Is there an audioguide in English?	râhnamâye sôti be zabâne ingilisi dârid?	راهنمای صوتی به زبان انگلیسی دارید؟
How much is admission?	vorudi chande?	ورودی چنده؟
Visiting hours	sâate bâzdid	ساعات بازدید
Open	bâz	باز
Closed	ta'til	تعطیل
Free admission	vorud râyegân	ورود رایگان
No flash photography	akâsi bâ felâsh mamnu' ast	عکاسی با فلاش ممنوع است
Staff only	faghat persenel	فقط پرسنل
Do not touch	dast nazanid	دست نزنید
built in	sâkhte shode dar …	ساخته شده در ...

At the museum		در موزه /dar muze/
English	**Pronunciation**	**Persian**
founded in	ta'sis shode dar …	... تأسیس شده در
painter	naghâsh	نقاش
masterpiece	shâhkâr	شاهکار
display	namâyeshgâh	نمایشگاه
king	shâh	شاه
queen	malake	ملکه
Photo taking	aksbardâri	عکسبرداری
Could I take pictures here?	mitunam injâ aks begiram?	می تونم اینجا عکس بگیرم؟
Could I use a flash?	mitunam az felâsh estefâde konam?	می تونم از فلاش استفاده کنم؟

Camping		اردو زدن /ordu zadan/
English	**Pronunciation**	**Persian**
Is there a campsite nearby?	in atrâf jâyi barâye ordu hast?	این اطراف جایی برای اردو هست؟
May we camp out here?	momkene injâ ordu bezanim?	ممکنه اینجا اردو بزنیم.
Do you have space for a tent?	barâye ye châdor jâ dârid?	برای یه چادر جا دارید؟
What is the charge per day?	hazineye ruzâne chande?	هزینه روزانه چنده؟
What is the charge for a tent?	hazineye ye châdor chande?	هزینه یه چادر چنده؟

Camping		اردو زدن /ordu zadan/
English	**Pronunciation**	**Persian**
What is the charge for a trailer?	hazineye ye kârâvân chande?	هزینه یه کاراوان چنده؟
What is the charge for a car?	hazineye ye mâshin chande?	هزینه یه ماشین چنده؟
Are there electrical outlets on site?	injâ pirize bargh hast?	اینجا پریز برق هست؟
Are there trash cans on site?	injâ satle zobâle hast?	اینجا سطل زباله هست؟
Are there showers on site?	injâ dush hast?	اینجا دوش هست؟
Where can I get some drinking water?	kojâ mitunam kami âbe khordan peidâ konam?	کجا می تونم کمی آب خوردن پیدا کنم؟
Is the town far from here?	shahr az injâ kheili dure?	شهر از اینجا خیلی دوره؟
Is fishing allowed here?	injâ mâhigiri mojâze?	اینجا ماهیگیری مجازه؟
Is hunting allowed here?	injâ shekâr mojâze?	اینجا شکار مجازه؟
It's too crowded here.	injâ kheyli sholughe	اینجا خیلی شلوغه
The ground's too uneven.	zamin kheyli nâhamvâre	زمین خیلی ناهمواره
I would like a map of the walking trails in this region.	man ye naghsheye masirâye piyâderavi in mantaghe ro mikhâm	من یه نقشه مسیرهای پیاده روی این منطقه رو می خوام.
sleeping pad	toshakche	تشکچه
camp fire	âtash	آتش
campground	ordugâh	اردوگاه

Camping		اردو زدن /ordu zadan/
English	Pronunciation	Persian
Drinking water	âbe âshâmidani	آب آشامیدنی
matches	kebrit	کبریت
charcoal	zoghâl	زغال
tent pole	tire châdor	تیر چادر
hammer	chakosh	چکش
tent pegs	mikhe châdor	میخ چادر
kerosene stove	ojâghe nafti	اجاق نفتی
sleeping bag	kiseye khâb	کیسه خواب
ground cloth	zirandâz	زیرانداز

At the beach		در ساحل /dar sâhel/
English	Pronunciation	Persian
Can I go water-skiing there?	mitunam unjâ eski ruye âb konam?	می تونم اونجا اسکی روی آب کنم؟
Can I go diving there?	mitunam unjâ ghavâsi konam?	می تونم اونجا غواصی کنم؟
Where can I rent a motorboat?	kojâ mitunam ye ghâyeghe motori kerâye konam?	کجا می تونم یه قایق موتوری کرایه کنم؟
diving equipment	vasâyele ghavâsi	وسایل غواصی
umbrella	chatr	چتر

English	Pronunciation	Persian
Where is the nearest rental office?	nazdiktarin daftare kerâye kojâst?	نزدیکترین دفتر کرایه کجاست؟
diving center	markaze ghavâsi	مرکز غواصی
water park	pârke âbi	پارک آبی
How much does it cost to rent a boat?	hazineye kerâyeye ye ghâyegh chande?	هزینه کرایه یه قایق چنده؟
Is it necessary to put down a deposit?	vadi'e lâzeme?	ودیعه لازمه؟
When do I have to bring the boat back?	key bâyad ghâyegh ro bargardunam?	کی باید قایق رو برگردونم؟
Where can I find an instructor?	kojâ mitunam ye morabi peidâ konam?	کجا می تونم یه مربی پیدا کنم؟
What is the depth here?	omghe injâ cheghadre?	عمق اینجا چقدره؟
How can I get to the beach from here?	chetor mitunam az injâ be sâhel beram?	چه طور می تونم ازاینجا به ساحل برم؟
Is it safe to swim here?	injâ barâye shenâ bikhatare?	اینجا برای شنا کردن بی خطره؟
Is there an outdoor pool nearby?	in atrâf estakhre rubâz hast?	این اطراف استخر روباز هست؟
fitness center	markaze âmâdegiye jesmâni	مرکز آمادگی جسمانی

Countryside	خارج از شهر /khârej az shahr/	
English	Pronunciation	Persian
area, region	mantaghe	منطقه
beach	sâhel	ساحل
Bridge	pol	پل
canal	kânâl	کانال
cliff	sakhre	صخره
Desert	sahrâ	صحرا
desert	biyâbân	بیابان
earth, land	zamin	زمین
Farm	mazra'e	مزرعه
farm	mazra'e	مزرعه
Field	dasht	دشت
Flower	gol	گل
forest	jangal	جنگل
harbor	bandargâh	بندرگاه
hill	tape	تپه
island	jazire	جزیره
Jungle	jangal	جنگل
Lake	daryâche	دریاچه
Mountain	kuh	کوه
mountain	kuh	کوه

Countryside		خارج از شهر /khârej az shahr/
English	**Pronunciation**	**Persian**
ocean	oghyânus	اقیانوس
path	jâde	جاده
port	bandar	بندر
quay	eskele	اسکله
railway	râhâhan	راه آهن
Rain	bârân	باران
rock	sakhre	صخره
sand	shen	شن
scenery	cheshmandâz	چشم انداز
Sea	daryâ	دریا
seaside	kenâre daryâ	کنار دریا
sky	âsemân	آسمان
soil	khâk	خاک
Tree	derakht	درخت
valley	dare	دره
village	rustâ	روستا
waterfall	âbshâr	آبشار
wood	chub	چوب

Healthcare and Beauty Care

سلامتی زیبایی

/salâmati va zibâyi/

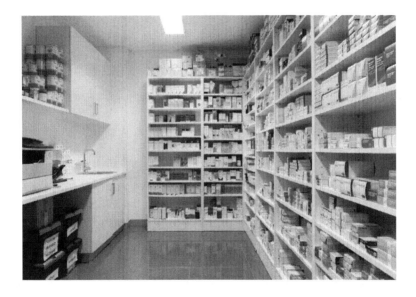

Drugstore		داروخانه /dârukhâne/
English	**Pronunciation**	**Persian**
Where is the nearest all-night drugstore?	nazdiktarin dârukhâneye shabâneruzi kojâst?	نزدیکترین داروخانه شبانه روزی کجاست؟
What time does the drugstore open?	darukhâne che sâati bâze?	داروخانه چه ساعتی بازه؟
What time does the drugstore close?	dârukhâne che sâati tatil mikone?	داروخانه چه ساعتی تعطیل می کنه؟
Can you make up this prescription for me?	momkene in noskharo barâye man bepichid?	ممکنه این نسخه رو برای من بپیچید؟
Shall I wait?	bâyad montazer bemunam?	باید منتظر بمونم؟
I will come back for it.	man barâye gereftanesh bar migardam	من برای گرفتنش بر می گردم.
Do I need a prescription for this?	barâye in bâyad noskhe dâshte bâsham?	برای این باید نسخه داشته باشم؟
Could I have something for a cough?	momkene chizi barâye sorfe be man bedid?	ممکنه چیزی برای سرفه به من بدید؟
Could I have something for sunburn?	momkene chizi barâye âftâb sukhtegi be man bedid?	ممکنه چیزی برای آفتاب سوختگی به من بدید؟
Could I have something for diarrhea?	momkene chizi barâye eshâl be man bedid?	ممکنه چیزی برای اسهال به من بدید؟
Could I have something for a hangover?	momkene chizi barâye kesâlate alekoli be man bedid?	ممکنه چیزی برای کسالت الکلی به من بدید؟

Drugstore		داروخانه /dârukhâne/
English	**Pronunciation**	**Persian**
Could I have something for an upset stomach?	momkene chizi barâye be ham khordan me'de be man bedid?	ممکنه چیزی برای به هم خوردن معده به من بدید؟
Could I have something for a sore throat?	momkene chizi barâye galudard be man bedid?	ممکنه چیزی برای گلو درد به من بدید؟
Could I have something for motion sickness?	momkene chizi barâye del be ham khordegiye nâshi az harkat be man bedid?	ممکنه چیزی برای دل به هم خوردگی ناشی از حرکت به من بدید؟
Could I have something for insect bites?	momkene chizi barâye gazidegiye hashare be man bedid?	ممکنه چیزی برای گزیدگی حشره به من بدید؟
Symptoms	alâeme bimâri	علائم بیماری
I don't feel well.	hâlam khub nist	حالم خوب نیست.
I have a pain in my throat.	galum dard mikone	گلوم درد می کنه.
I have a pain in my chest.	ghafaseye sinam dard mikone	قفسه سینم درد می کنه.
I have a pain in my side.	pahlum dard mikone	پهلوم درد می کنه.
I have a pain in my arm.	dastam dard mikone	دستم درد می کنه.
I feel dizzy.	ehsâse sargije dâram	احساس سرگیجه دارم.
I feel faint.	ehsâse za'f dâram	احساس ضعف دارم.
I feel sick.	ehsâs mikonam mariz shodam	احساس می کنم مریض شدم.
I have a fever.	man tab dâram	من تب دارم.

LearnPersianOnline.com

Drugstore		داروخانه /dârukhâne/
English	**Pronunciation**	**Persian**
I have a headache.	saram dard mikone	سرم درد می کنه.
I have a back pain.	kamaram dard mikone	کمرم درد می کنه.
I have a toothache.	dandunam dard mikone	دندونم درد می کنه.
I have a stomach ache.	me'dam dard mikone	معده ام درد می کنه.
I feel a little better.	kami behtaram	کمی بهتر هستم.
I have a bruise.	man zarb didam	من ضرب دیده ام.
I have a lump.	injâm bâd karde	اینجایم باد کرده
I have a burn.	man sukhtegi daram	من سوختگی دارم
I have a cut.	man boridegi ru badanam dâram	من بریدگی رو بدنم دارم.
I have a graze.	man kharâshidegi dâram	من خراشیدگی دارم.
I have a swelling.	man varam dâram	من ورم دارم.
I have a rash.	man dune zadam	من دونه زدم
I have asthma.	man âsm dâram	من آسم دارم.
I have constipation.	man yobusat dâram	من یبوست دارم.
I have hemorrhoids.	man bavâsir dâram	من بواسیر دارم.
I have the chills.	man larz dâram	من لرز دارم.
I have bronchitis.	man bronshit dâram	من برونشیت دارم.
It's a sharp pain.	darde shadid dâre	درد شدید داره.
It's a dull pain.	darde molâyemi dâre	درد ملایمی داره.

LearnPersianOnline.com

Drugstore داروخانه /dârukhâne/		
English	**Pronunciation**	**Persian**
It hurts constantly.	dâem dard mikone	دائم درد می کنه.
It only hurts now and then.	gâhi dard mikone	گاهی درد می کنه.
I have diarrhea.	man eshâl dâram	من اسهال دارم.
I have food poisoning.	man masmum shodam	من مسموم شدم.
I have pneumonia.	man zâtoriye dâram	من ذات الریه دارم.
I have the flu.	anfolânzâ	آنفولانزا
I have high blood pressure.	feshâre khune bâlâ	فشار خون بالا
I get headaches often.	man aghlab sardard dâram	من اغلب سر درد دارم.
It hurts more at night.	bishtar shabhâ dard mikone	بیشتر شبها درد می کنه.
I have a runny nose.	âbrizeshe bini dâram	آبریزش بینی دارم.
I have a stuffy nose.	binim gerefte	بینیم گرفته
I have an upset stomach.	me'dam be ham rikhte	معده ام به هم ریخته
My lymph nodes are swollen.	ghodade lanfâvim varam karde	غدد لنفاوی من ورم کرده
I banged my shoulder.	shunam zarb dide	شونم ضرب دیده
I banged my arm.	bâzum zarb dide	بازوم ضرب دیده
I banged my hand.	dastam zarb dide	دستم ضرب دیده
I banged my head.	saram zarb dide	سرم ضرب دیده
I dislocated my arm.	bâzuye man dar rafte	بازوی من در رفته

	Drugstore		داروخانه /dârukhâne/
English	**Pronunciation**		**Persian**
I dislocated my leg.	pâye man dar rafte		پای من در رفته
I dislocated my finger.	angoshte daste man dar rafte		انگشت دست من در رفته
I dislocated my toe.	angoshte pâye man dar rafte		انگشت پای من در رفته
I have broken my arm.	bâzuye man shekaste		بازوی من شکسته
I have broken my leg.	pâye man shekaste		پای من شکسته
I have broken my finger.	angoshte daste man shekaste		انگشت دست من شکسته
I have broken my toe.	angoshte pâye man shekaste		انگشت پای من شکسته
I banged my knee.	zânum zarb dide		زانوم ضرب دیده
I sprained my ankle.	moche pâm rag be rag shode		مچ پایم رگ به رگ شده
I twisted my ankle.	moche pâm pich khorde		مچ پام پیچ خورده
I have got a bad case of athlete's foot.	man bimâriye ghârchiye angoshtâye pâ gereftam		من بیماری قارچی انگشتان پا گرفتم
I have got a heart problem.	man bimâriye ghalbi dâram		من بیماری قلبی دارم
I have something in my eye.	tuye cheshmam chizi rafte		توی چشمم چیزی رفته
I'm suffering from insomnia.	man moshkele bikhâbi dâram		من مشکل بی خوابی دارم
I lost weight.	man lâghar shodam		من لاغر شدم.
I am seasick.	daryâzade shodam		دریازده شدم.

Drugstore		داروخانه /dârukhâne/
English	Pronunciation	Persian
I am car sick.	mâshinzade shodam	ماشین زده شدم.
I am diabetic.	man diyâbet dâram	من دیابت دارم.
I was bitten.	ye chizi mano gazide	یه چیزی منو گزیده
cold	sarmâ khordegi	سرما خوردگی
fever	tab	تب
How often should I take the medicine?	in dâru ro bâyad har chand vaght yekbâr masraf konam?	این دارو رو باید هر چند وقت یکبار مصرف کنم؟
How should this medicine be taken?	in dâru bâyad chetor masraf beshe?	این دارو باید چه طور مصرف بشه؟
On an empty stomach?	bâ me'deye khâli?	با معده خالی؟
After meals?	ba'd az ghazâ?	بعد از غذا؟
Before meals?	ghabl az ghazâ?	قبل از غذا؟
With meals?	bâ ghazâ?	با غذا؟
Is it suitable for children?	barâye bachehâ monâsebe?	برای بچه ها مناسبه؟
Are there any side effects associated with this medicine?	in dâru avâreze jânebi dâre?	این دارو عوارض جانبی داره؟
I would like a bottle of aspirin.	man ye ghuti âsperin mikhâm	من یه قوطی آسپرین می خوام.
Could I have some aspirin?	momkene âsperin be man bedid?	ممکنه آسپرین به من بدید؟

Could I have some antiseptic cream?	momkene kereme zede âftâb be man bedid?	ممکنه کرم ضدعفونی به من بدید؟
Could I have some insect repellent?	momkene dâfe'e hasharât be man bedid?	ممکنه دافع حشرات به من بدید؟
Could I have some condoms?	momkene kândom be man bedid?	ممکنه کاندوم به من بدید؟
Could I have some toothpaste?	momkene khamir dandun be man bedid?	ممکنه خمیر دندون به من بدید؟
Could I have some tissues?	momkene dastmâl kâghazi be man bedid?	ممکنه دستمال کاغذی به من بدید؟
Expiration date	târikhe enghezâ	تاریخ انقضا
For external use only	faghat barâye estemâle khâreji	فقط برای استعمال خارجی
Not to be taken internally	barâye estemâle dâkheli nist	برای استعمال داخلی نیست
Requires a doctor's prescription	forush bâ noskheye pezeshk	فروش با نسخه پزشک
intravenous	darun varidi	درون وریدی
rectal	magh'adi	مقعدی
oral	dahâni	دهانی
teaspoon	ghâshoghe châykhori	قاشق چایخوری
dosage	meghdâre masraf	مقدار مصرف
pill , tablet	ghors	قرص
coated tablet	ghorse pusheshdâr	قرص پوشش دار
effervescent tablets	ghorshâye jushân	قرص های جوشان
pastille	mekidani	مکیدنی

capsule	kapsul	کپسول
ampoule	âmpul	آمپول
drops	ghatre	قطره
liniment	roghane mâlidani	روغن مالیدنی
mixture	makhlut	مخلوط
syrup	sharbat	شربت
suppository	shiyâf	شیاف
powder	pudr	پودر
solution	mahlul	محلول
cream	kerem	کرم
remedy	darmân	درمان
drug	dâru	دارو
painkiller	dâruye mosaken	داروی مسکن
tranquilizer , sedative	ârâmbakhsh	آرام بخش
sleeping pills	ghorse khâb	قرص خواب
non-aspirin substitute	mosakeni gheir az âspirin	مسکنی غیر از آسپرین
cough drops	ghatreye sorfe	قطره سرفه
ear drops	ghatreye gush	قطره گوش
eye drops	ghatreye cheshm	قطره چشم
sterilizing solution	mahlule estril konande	محلول استریل کننده
cleaning solution	mahlule pâk konande	محلول پاک کننده
soaking solution	mahlule khisândan	محلول خیساندن

anti-allergy pills	ghorse zede âlerzhi	قرص ضد آلرژی
anti-asthma spray	espereye zede âsm	اسپری ضد آسم
thermometer	daraje	درجه
roll bandages	bând	باند
adhesive plaster	chasbe zakhm	چسب زخم
moisturizing cream	kereme martub konande	کرم مرطوب کننده
hand cream	kereme dast	کرم دست
balm	pâmâd	پماد
dental floss	nakhe dandun	نخ دندون
toothbrush	mesvâk	مسواک
suntan cream/lotion	kerem barâye hamâme âftâb	کرم برای حمام آفتاب
sun block	kereme zede âftâb	کرم ضد آفتاب
razor blades	tighe surat tarâshi	تیغ صورت تراشی
aftershave	aftersheyv	افترشیو
toilet paper	dastmâle tuâlet	دستمال توالت
soap	sâbun	صابون
sanitary napkins	navâre behdâshti	نوار بهداشتی
comb	shâne	شانه
conditioner	narmkonande	نرم کننده
hair spray	espereye mu	اسپری مو
shampoo	shâmpu	شامپو
diapers	pushak	پوشک

	Pain	درد /dard/
English	**Pronunciation**	**Persian**
cold	sarmâkhordegi	سرماخوردگی
cough	sorfe	سرفه
period cramps	darde heyz	درد حیض
headache	sardard	سردرد
chills	larz	لرز
sore throat	galudard	گلودرد
dizziness	sargije	سرگیجه
abdominal pains	shekam dard	شکم درد
burn	sukhtegi	سوختگی
cut	boridegi	بریدگی
graze	kharâshidegi	خراشیدگی
swelling	varam	ورم
flu	ânfolânzâ	آنفولانزا
boil	damal	دمل
fracture	shekastegi	شکستگی
strain	keshidegiye azole	کشیدگی عضله
blister	tâval	تاول
wound	jerâhat	جراحت
bruise	kabudi	کبودی
lump	barâmadegi	برآمدگی

	Pain	درد /dard/
English	**Pronunciation**	**Persian**
rash	dâne	دانه
insect bite	nishe hashare	نیش حشره
stiff neck	gereftegiye gardan	گرفتگی گردن
migraine headache	sardarde migreni	سردرد میگرنی

	Seeing a doctor	مراجعه به پزشک /morâje'e be pezeshk/
English	**Pronunciation**	**Persian**
I would like to see a doctor.	man mikhâm ye pezeshk mano bebine	من می خوام پزشک منو ببینه
I would like to make an appointment.	man mikhâm ye vaght begiram	من می خوام یه وقت بگیرم.
I need a medical consultation.	man niyâz be moshâvereye pezeshki dâram	من نیاز به مشاوره پزشکی دارم.
What are the consultation hours?	moshâvere che sâatiye?	مشاوره چه ساعتیه؟
Where is the nearest eye specialist?	nazdiktarin motekhasese cheshm kojâst?	نزدیکترین متخصص چشم کجاست؟
throat specialist	motekhasese halgh	متخصص حلق
ear specialist	motekhasese gush	متخصص گوش
Is it contagious?	mosriye?	مسریه؟
Is it dangerous?	khatarnâke?	خطرناکه؟
Can you give me something to stop the pain?	momkene chizi barâye ghat' shodane dard be man bedid?	ممکنه چیزی برای قطع شدن درد به من بدید؟

Seeing a doctor		مراجعه به پزشک /morâje'e be pezeshk/
English	**Pronunciation**	**Persian**
I have previously received treatment for an ulcer.	man ghablan be khâtere zakhme me'de tahte darmân budam.	من قبلاً به خاطر زخم معده تحت درمان بودم
My blood type is 0 positive.	goruhe khuniye man oye mosbate	گروه خونی من O مثبته
My blood type is 0 negative.	o manfi	Oمنفی
My blood type is A negative.	â manfi	Aمنفی
My blood type is B negative.	be manfi	Bمنفی
My blood type is A positive.	â mosbat	Aمثبت
My blood type is B positive.	be mosbat	Bمثبت
My blood type is AB positive.	âbe mosbat	ABمثبت
My blood type is AB negative.	âbe manfi	ABمنفی
I'm nearsighted.	man nazdikbin hastam	من نزدیک بین هستم.
I am taking this medicine.	man az in dâru estefâde mikonam	من از این دارو استفاده می کنم.
I am on a diet.	man rezhim dâram	من رژیم دارم.
What's my temperature?	damâye badane man cheghadre?	دمای بدن من چقدره؟
How long will it take to recover?	cheghadr tul mikeshe khub sham?	چقدر طول می کشه خوب شم؟

LearnPersianOnline.com

Seeing a doctor		مراجعه به پزشک /morâje'e be pezeshk/
English	**Pronunciation**	**Persian**
Can I continue my trip?	mitunam be safaram edâme bedam?	می تونم به سفرم ادامه بدم؟
Can you please let my family know?	momkene lotfan be khânevâdam etelâ' bedid?	ممکنه لطفاً به خانوادم اطلاع بدید؟
I'm Persianghted.	man durbin hastam	من دوربین هستم.
I have missed a period.	man ye mâhe periyod nashodam	من یه ماهه پریود نشدم.
I am pregnant.	man bârdâr hastam	من باردار هستم.
Am I allowed to get out of bed?	ejâze dâram takhtekhâb ro tark konam?	اجازه دارم تختخواب رو ترک کنم؟
Would you please write me a prescription for a tranquilizer?	momkene barâye man ye ârambakhsh benevisid?	ممکنه برای من یه آرام بخش بنویسید؟
Where's the X-ray room?	otâghe râdiolozhi kojâst?	اتاق رادیولوژی کجاست؟
How much will this test cost?	in âzmâyesh cheghadr hazine dâre?	این آزمایش چقدر هزینه داره؟
appointment	vaghte ta'in shode	وقت تعیین شده
examination/check-up	moâyene	معاینه
prescription	noskhe	نسخه
treatment	darmân	درمان
analysis	âzmâyesh	آزمایش
X-ray	asha'eye iks	اشعه ایکس

Seeing a doctor		مراجعه به پزشک /morâje'e be pezeshk/
English	**Pronunciation**	**Persian**
physical examination	moâyeneye jesmi	معاینه جسمی
nurse	parastâr	پرستار
indigestion	suehâzeme	سوء هاضمه
infection	ofunat	عفونت
nausea	hâlate tahavo'	حالت تهوع
urinary infection	ofunate majâriye edrâr	عفونت مجاری ادرار
venereal disease	bimâriye moghârebati	بیماری مقاربتی
worms	kerm	کرم
arthritis	ârteroz	آرتروز
specimen	nemuneye âzmâyesh	نمونه آزمایش
asthma	âsm	آسم
bronchitis	bronshit	برونشیت
allergy	hasâsiyat	حساسیت
heart disease	bimâriye ghalbi	بیماری قلبی

	Dentist	دندانپزشک /dandânpezeshk/
English	**Pronunciation**	**Persian**
I need to see a dentist.	man bâyad pishe dandânpezeshk beram	من باید پیش یه دندانپزشک بروم.
Where is the nearest dental clinic?	nazdiktarin kilinike dandânpezeshki kojâst?	نزدیکترین کلینیک دندانپزشکی کجاست؟
I have lost a filling.	porshodegiye dandânam kande shode	پرشدگی دندونم کنده شده
It hurts when I chew.	vaghti ghazâ mijoam dard migire	وقتی غذا می جوم درد می گیره
I have lost a tooth.	ye dandune man oftâde	یه دندون من افتاده
My gums hurt.	lasehâm dard mikonan	لثه هام درد می کنن
Don't pull it out.	in dandun ro nakeshid	این دندون رو نکشید.
Please, do something for the pain.	lotfan barâye darde un kâri konid	لطفاً برای درد اون کاری کنید.
Can you fix my dentures?	mituni dandunâye masnu'iye mano dorost konid?	می تونید دندونای مصنوعی منو درست کنید؟
Please, crown this tooth.	lotfan in dandun ro rukesh konid	لطفاً این دندون رو روکش کنید.

Hair salon		آرایشگاه /ârâyeshgâh/
English	Pronunciation	Persian
bangs	muye chatri	موی چتری
beauty salon	sâlone zibâyi	سالن زیبایی
carving	fere kutâh modat	فر کوتاه مدت
conditioning treatment	negahdâriye mu	نگهداری مو
curls	fer	فر
hairdresser's	ârâyeshgâh	آرایشگاه
highlights	hâylâyt	هایلایت
makeup	ârâyesh	آرایش
nail extension	nâkhone masnu'i	ناخن مصنوعی
spa	âbegarm	آبگرم
stylist	ârâyeshgar	آرایشگر
tint	rang	رنگ
Do you do hair removal?	shomâ epilâsiyon mikonid?	شما اپیلاسیون می کنید؟
I want to have a skin treatment.	lotfan pustam ro tamiz konid	لطفاً پوستم رو تمیز کنید.
I would like you to file and shape my nails.	man mikhâm nâkhunâmo shekl bedid va lâk bezanid	من می خوام ناخنهام رو شکل بدید و لاک بزنید.
classic manicure	mânikore kelâsik	مانیکور کلاسیک
cleaning	pâk kardan	پاک کردن/تمیز کردن
epilation	epilâsiyon	اپیلاسیون
mask	mâsk	ماسک

LearnPersianOnline.com

Hair salon		آرایشگاه /ârâyeshgâh/
English	**Pronunciation**	**Persian**
massage	mâsâzh	ماساژ
nail repair	tarmime nâkhon	ترمیم ناخن
pedicure	pedikor	پدیکور
peeling	piling	پیلینگ
I would like to make an appointment for a haircut.	man mikhâm barâye kutâh kardane mu vaght begiram	من می خوام برای کوتاه کردن مو وقت بگیرم.
How long will I have to wait?	che modat bâyad montazer bemunam?	چه مدت باید منتظر بمونم؟
Where can I sit down?	kojâ mitunam beshinam?	کجا می تونم بنشینم؟
Please cut and blow-dry my hair.	lotfan muye mano kotâh konid va seshvâr bekeshid	لطفاً موی منو کوتاه کنید و سشوار بکشید.
Please shampoo and style my hair.	lotfan muye mano shâmpu bezanid va model bedid	لطفاً موی منو شامپو بزنید و مدل بدید
I would like to have a haircut.	man mikhâm muhâmo kutâh konam	من می خوام موهام رو کوتاه کنم.
I want to have a hairdo.	man mikhâm be muye man model bedid	من می خوام به موی من مدل بدید
I want to have a shampoo.	man mikhâm shâmpu bezanam	من می خوام شامپو بزنم.
I want to have a facial.	man mikhâm mâske surat bezâram	من می خوام ماسک صورت بذارم

Hair salon		آرایشگاه /ârâyeshgâh/
English	**Pronunciation**	**Persian**
I want to have a waxing.	man mikhâm epilâsiyon konam	من می خوام اپیلاسیون کنم.
I want to have my hair cut.	lotfan muye mano kutâh konid	لطفاً موی منو کوتاه کنید.
I want to have my hair curled.	lotfan muye mano fer konid	لطفاً موی منو فر کنید.
I want to have my hair colored.	lotfan muye mano rang konid	لطفاً موی منو رنگ کنید.
Cut it short, please.	lotfan kutâsh konid	لطفاً کوتاش کنید.
Just a trim, please.	lotfan faghat moratabesh konid	لطفاً فقط مرتبش کنید.
Just take some off the edges.	faghat kami az atrâf ro kutâh konid	فقط کمی از اطراف رو کوتاه کنید.
Please trim my beard.	lotfan rishe man ro kutâh konid	لطفاً ریش من رو کوتاه کنید.
Please trim my moustache.	lotfan sibile man ro kutâh konid	لطفاً سبیل من رو کوتاه کنید.
Not too short.	kheyli kutâh nashe	خیلی کوتاه نشه
A soft perm, please.	ye fere dâeme narm lotfan	یه فر دائم نرم، لطفاً.
Please blow-dry my hair.	lotfan muye mano bâ seshvâr khoshk konid	لطفاً موی منو با سشوار خشک کنید.
I want a short cut.	man modele muye kutâh mikhâm	من مدل موی کوتاه می خوام.

Please curl the ends inward.	lotfan pâyine mu ro be dâkhel fer konid	لطفاً پایین مو رو به داخل فر کنید.
Please curl the ends outward.	lotfan pâyine mu ro be birun fer konid	لطفاً پایین مو رو به بیرون فر کنید.
Please part my hair in the middle.	lotfan farghe mano az vasat bâz konid	لطفاً فرق منو از وسط باز کنید.
Please part my hair on the right side.	lotfan farghe mano az samte râst bâz konid	لطفاً فرق منو از سمت راست باز کنید.
Please fix the style with hair spray.	lotfan modele mu ro bâ espereye mu sâbet konid	لطفاً مدل مو رو با اسپری مو ثابت کنید.
Without hair spray, please.	lotfan bedune espereye mu	لطفاً بدون اسپری مو.
I would like to have my scalp massaged.	lotfan puste saram ro mâsâzh bedid	لطفاً پوست سرم رو ماساژ بدید.

Emergencies

وضعیت اضطراری
/vaz'iyate ezterâri/

Accidents		حوادث /havâdes/
English	**Pronunciation**	**Persian**
Please call a doctor.	lotfan ye doktor khabar konid	.لطفاً یه دکتر خبر کنید
Please call an ambulance.	lotfan ye âmbolâns khabar konid	.لطفاً یه آمبولانس خبر کنید
Take me to a hospital!	mano be bimârestân bebarid!	!منو به بیمارستان ببرید
He is unconscious.	u bihushe	او بیهوشه
He is seriously injured.	u shadidan sadame dide	او شدیداً صدمه دیده
I'm bleeding.	man khunrizi dâram	.من خونریزی دارم
He's bleeding.	u khunrizi dâre	.او خونریزی داره
I was hit by a car.	man bâ ye mâshin tasâdof kardam	.من با یه ماشین تصادف کردم
I have lost a lot of blood.	meghdâre ziyâdi khun az man rafte	مقدار زیادی خون از من رفته
I tripped on the steps.	tuye pelehâ pâm gir kard va oftâdam	توی پله ها پایم گیر کرد و افتادم
I fell down the stairs.	man az pelehâ oftâdam	.من از پله ها افتادم
Do I have to stay in the hospital?	bâyad tu bimârestân bemunam?	باید تو بیمارستان بمونم؟
Here is my medical insurance policy.	befarmâyid in bime nâmeye pezeshkiye mane	بفرمایید این بیمه نامه پزشکی منه
Do I need an operation?	niyâz be amale jarâhi dâram?	نیاز به عمل جراحی دارم؟
Will I need local anesthesia?	bihushiye moze'i barâye man lâzeme?	بیهوشی موضعی برای من لازمه؟

Accidents		حوادث /havâdes/
English	**Pronunciation**	**Persian**
I'm allergic to penicillin.	man be penisilin hasâsiyat dâram	من به پنی سیلین حساسیت دارم.
I'm allergic to antibiotics.	man be ântibiyutik hasâsiyat dâram	من به آنتی بیوتیک حساسیت دارم.
I have a reaction to novocaine.	man be dâruye bihushi ... hasâsiyat dâram	... من به داروی بیهوشی حساسیت دارم.
I'm not allergic to any drugs.	man be hich dâruyi hasâsiyat nadâram	من به هیچ دارویی حساسیت ندارم.
I took these pills.	man in ghorsâro mikhoram	من این قرص ها رو می خورم.
I'm allergic.	man hasâsiyat dâram	من حساسیت دارم.
I'm epileptic.	man sar' dâram	من صرع دارم.
I'm disabled.	man ma'luliyat dâram	من معلولیت دارم.

Police		پلیس /polis/
English	**Pronunciation**	**Persian**
Help!	komak	کمک!
I need an interpreter.	man be ye motarjem niyâz dâram	من به یه مترجم نیاز دارم.
I lost my passport.	man gozarnâmamo gom kardam	من گذرنامه ام رو گم کردم
I lost my ticket.	man belitam ro gom kardam	من بلیطم رو گم کردم.

I lost my baggage.	man vasâyelam ro gom kardam	من وسایلم رو گم کردم.
I lost my purse.	man kifamo gom kardam	من کیفم رو گم کردم.
My passport was stolen.	gozarnâmeye man dozdide shode	گذرنامه من دزدیده شده
My ticket was stolen.	belite man dozdide shode	بلیط من دزدیده شده
My baggage was stolen.	vasâyele man dozdide shode	وسایل من دزدیده شدن
My purse was stolen.	kife man dozdide shode	کیف من دزدیده شده
My camera	durbine man	دوربین من
My watch	sâate mochiye man	ساعت مچی من
I need to call the embassy.	man bâyad bâ sefâratkhâne tamâs begiram	من باید با سفارتخانه تماس بگیرم.
I need to call my lawyer.	man bâyad bâ vakilam tamâs begiram	من باید با وکیلم تماس بگیرم.
I need to call my friends.	man bâyad bâ dustâm tamâs begiram	من باید با دوستانم تماس بگیرم.
Where is the lost-and-found?	daftar ashyâye gom shode kojâst?	دفتر اشیاء پیدا شده کجاست؟

Other books of Interest

Farsi Conversations
Learn the Most Common Words
and Phrases Farsi Speakers use Every Day

Learning about a new culture is always an exciting prospect and one of the best ways to get to know about another country, its people and their customs, is to learn the language.

Now, with Farsi Conversations: Learn the Most Common Words and Phrases Farsi Speakers use Every Day you can learn how to communicate in Farsi and learn more about Persian culture at the same time.

In this unique guide, you will be able to practice your spoken Farsi with FREE YouTube videos. It is an ideal tool for learners of Farsi at all levels, whether at school, in evening classes or at home, and is a 'must have' for business or leisure.

Farsi students can learn;

- How to use the right language structures and idioms in the right context
- Practice Farsi vocabulary and phrases needed in everyday situations
- Gain proficiency in written and spoken Farsi
- New ways of mastering Farsi phrases

By the end of the book you will have learned more than 2500 Farsi words, have mastered more than 300 commonly used Farsi verbs, key expressions and phrases and be able to pose more than 800 questions.

Purchase on Amazon website:

https://goo.gl/bGpVNZ

Published By:

Learn**Persian**Online.com

Learn to Speak Persian Fast: For Intermediate

Learn to Speak Persian Fast is a multi-level series for Persian learners from the beginning to the advanced level. It is a breakthrough in Persian language learning — offering a winning formula and the most powerful methods for learning to speak Persian fluently and confidently. Each book provides 10 chapters covering a comprehensive range of topics. Each chapter includes vocabulary, grammar, reading and writing lessons. There is a series of exercises that gives you extra practice in using new concepts and inspires you to construct personalized conversations.

Book 2 of *Learn to Speak Persian Fast* series builds on the foundations established in the book one for smooth and accurate communication in Persian. It is designed for intermediate students needing a comprehensive approach to learn grammar structures and vocabulary. It gives learners easy access to the Persian vocabulary and grammar as it is actually used in a comprehensive range of everyday life situations and it teaches students to use Persian for situations related to work, social life, and leisure. Topics such as weather, sports, transportation, customs, etc. are presented in interesting unique ways using real-life information. Beautiful illustrations enable students learn vocabulary and grammar lessons effectively.

The Only Book to Master Persian Language!

Purchase on Amazon website:

https://goo.gl/68p476

Published By:

LearnPersianOnline.com

Learn to Speak Persian Fast: For Advanced

Learn to Speak Persian Fast is a multi-level series for Persian learners from the beginning to the advanced level. It is a breakthrough in Persian language learning — offering a winning formula and the most powerful methods for learning to speak Persian fluently and confidently. Each book provides 10 chapters covering a comprehensive range of topics. Each chapter includes vocabulary, grammar, reading and writing lessons. There is a series of exercises that gives you extra practice in using new concepts and inspires you to construct personalized conversations.

Book 3 of *Learn to Speak Persian Fast* series builds on the foundations established in the book one and two for smooth and accurate communication in Persian. It is designed for upper-intermediate and advanced students needing a comprehensive approach to learn grammar structures and vocabulary. It gives learners easy access to the Persian vocabulary and grammar as it is actually used in a comprehensive range of everyday life situations and it teaches students to use Persian for situations related to work, social life, and leisure. Topics such as weather, sports, transportation, customs, etc. are presented in interesting unique ways using real-life information. Beautiful illustrations enable students learn vocabulary and grammar lessons effectively. At the same time, it provides more opportunities to develop reading and writing abilities, as well as more challenging content to develop students' higher-level thinking skills.

The Only Book to Master Persian Language!

Purchase on Amazon website:

https://goo.gl/V2wmJd

Published By:

LearnPersianOnline.com

101 Most Common Farsi Proverbs
and
Their Best English Equivalents

Provided specifically for Farsi learners at the advanced level, this book looks at the most colorful and entertaining area of Farsi vocabulary –proverbs. Persians love to use proverbs, phrases that are colorful and mysterious. The Essential proverbs in Persian offer an additional look at the idiomatic phrases and sayings that make Persian the rich language that it is.

This book will appeal to Farsi students at advanced level who want to understand and use the Farsi really used by native speakers. A compilation of 101 most popular Farsi proverbs widely used in Iran in everyday context with their best English equivalents are presented with illustrations so that learners using this section will have many idioms 'at their fingertips'.

Farsi proverbs in this book is a supplementary text for advanced students and professionals who want to better understand Farsi native speakers, publications and media. It's especially for those who have learned Farsi outside of Iran. If you already speak Farsi, but now would like to start speaking even better, then this book is just for you.

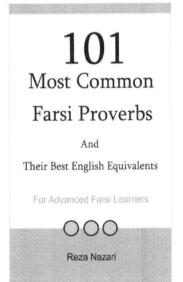

Purchase on Amazon website:

  https://goo.gl/guEmx3

Published By:

Learn**Persian**Online.com

Essential Idioms in Farsi

Learn The Most Common Farsi Idioms
Quickly and Effectively!

Written specifically for Farsi learners at the intermediate and advanced level, this reference book looks at the most colorful and entertaining area of Farsi vocabulary - idioms.

Persians love to use idioms, phrases that are colorful and mysterious. The Essential Idioms in Farsi offers an additional look at the idiomatic phrases and sayings that make Farsi the rich language that it is.

This book will appeal to students at advanced level who want to understand and use the Farsi really used by native speakers. Over 1,600 of the most-used Farsi idioms and phrases, which Farsi learners are likely to encounter are presented with illustrations so that learners using this book will have hundreds of idioms 'at their fingertips'.

Essential Idioms in Farsi is a supplementary text for advanced students and professionals who want to better understand Farsi native speakers, publications and media. It's especially for those who have learned Farsi outside of Iran. If you already speak Farsi, but now would like to start speaking even better, then this book is just for you.

Purchase on Amazon website:

https://goo.gl/8GEwgN

Published By:

LearnPersianOnline.com

Farsi Verbs Dictionary

The verb is an essential element of Farsi language - only the nouns occur more frequently in the written and spoken language. Verbs have always been a major problem for students no matter what system or approach the teacher uses.

Farsi verbs are usually found scattered in Farsi training books and they are difficult to find quickly when needed. This dictionary was prepared for English people interested in Farsi language. With a stunningly array of more than 3,000 entries, it is an invaluable work of reference.

The Farsi Verbs Dictionary is intended to serve as a guidebook on the meanings of all verbs you are most likely to read, hear, and use. The authors attempted to include all the verbs you are likely to need.

The main form of each verb given in the dictionary is the accepted Iranian standard spelling. Although there is usually one way that most verbs can be spelled, sometimes other spellings are also acceptable. However, the spelling given as the headword is the most that most people use.

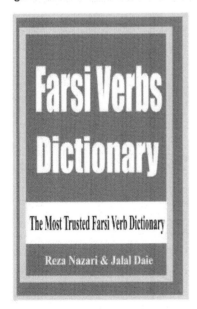

Purchase on Amazon website:

https://goo.gl/FQXH1R

Published By:
LearnPersianOnline.com

Persian for Travel

English - Persian Travel Phrases:
Start Speaking Persian Today!

This Book is for people who need to be able to communicate confidently and effectively when travelling. Typical situations covered are: at an airport, checking into a hotel, seeing a doctor, booking tickets and changing arrangements.

The emphasis is on understanding authentic Persian; on practicing the structures necessary to ask questions and check information and on extracting information from brochures, regulations and instructions. Vocabulary is clearly illustrated in context, and American English variants are provided.

"*Persian for Travel*" effortlessly teaches all the essential phrases you'll need to know before your trip. This book can be used as a self-study course - you do not need to work with a teacher. (It can also be used with a teacher). You don't even need to know a little Farsi before starting.

Purchase on Amazon website:

https://goo.gl/PMfdPL

Published By:
LearnPersianOnline.com

Farsi Grammar in Use

For Intermediate Students
An Easy-to-Use Guide with Clear Rules and Real-World Examples

Farsi Grammar in Use is an entertaining guide to Farsi grammar and usage. This user-friendly resource includes simple explanations of grammar and useful examples to help students of all ages improve their Farsi.

Farsi Grammar in Use is written for students who find the subjects unusually difficult and confusing -or in many cases, just plain boring. It doesn't take a lifetime to master Farsi grammar. All it takes is Farsi Grammar in Use. Filled with clear examples and self-assessment quizzes, this is one of the most highly trusted Farsi language resources available.

Farsi Grammar in Use is the only grammar Book You'll ever need! It can be used as a self-study course - you do not need to work with a teacher. (It can also be used with a teacher).

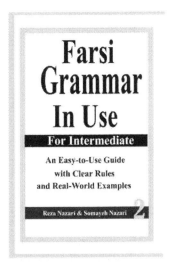

Purchase on Amazon website:

https://goo.gl/Hcx2Ij

Published By:
LearnPersianOnline.com

100 Short Stories in Persian

Designed for Persian lovers at the intermediate and advanced level, this book offers 100 fun, interesting, and appealing short stories. The stories motivate you to enjoy reading enthusiastically. 100 Short Stories in Persian contains simple yet entertaining stories to help you improve your Persian reading and writing skills by covering a diverse range of grammar structures and vocabulary.

Reading short stories is probably the best way for most Persian lovers to improve their Persian conveniently. If you're learning Persian and love reading, this is the book you need to take your Persian to the next level.

This book comes with a Persian and English glossary, so you can find the meaning of keywords in stories.

Best Short Stories to Grow Your Vocabulary

and Improve Your Pesian!

Purchase on Amazon website:

https://goo.gl/16r36Q

Published By:

Learn**Persian**Online.com

Persia Club Dictionary Farsi - English (Persian Edition)

Designed for people interested in learning standard Farsi, this comprehensive dictionary of the Farsi-English languages contains more than 12,000 entries and definitions as well as pronunciation guides, word types, Current phrases, slang, idioms, scientific terms and other features.

The Dictionary is fully updated with the latest lexical content. It's a unique database that offers the fullest, most accurate picture of the Farsi language today. Hundreds of new words cover technology, computing, ecology, and many other subjects.

• A comprehensive Farsi - English dictionary
• Fully updated with the latest lexical content
• Offers more than 12,000 Farsi entries
• A unique database that offers the fullest, most accurate picture of the Farsi language today
• Contains pronunciation guides, word types, slangs, idioms, scientific terms and other features
• Hundreds of new words cover technology, computing, ecology, and many other subjects.

An excellent reference resource for Persian learners to have on-hand!

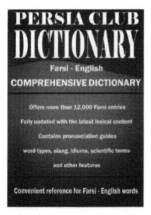

The Best Persian - English Dictionary!

Published By:

LearnPersianOnline.com

Purchase on Amazon website:

https://goo.gl/ofHCF8

Top 1,500 Persian Words

Essential Words for Communicating in Persian

Designed as a quick reference and study guide, this reference book provides easy-to-learn lists of the most relevant Persian vocabulary. Arranged by 36 categories, these word lists furnish the reader with an invaluable knowledge of fundamental vocabulary to comprehend, read, write and speak Persian.

Top 1,500 Persian Words is intended to teach the essentials of Persian quickly and effectively. The common words are organized to enable the reader to handle day-to-day situations. Words are arranged by topic, such as Family, Jobs, weather, numbers, countries, sports, common verbs, etc. A phonetic pronunciation accompanies each word.

With daily practice, you can soon have a working vocabulary in Persian!

The book "*Top 1,500 Persian Words*" is incredibly useful for those who want to learn Persian language **quickly** and **efficiently.**

Learn Most Common Persian Words FAST!

Purchase on Amazon website:

https://goo.gl/YvhpKe

Published By:

Learn**Persian**Online.com

Learn to Speak Persian Online

Enjoy interactive Persian lessons on Skype
with the best native speaking Persian teachers

Online Persian Learning that's Effective, Affordable, Flexible, and Fun.

Learn Persian wherever you want; when you want

Ultimate flexibility. You can now learn Persian online via Skype, enjoy high quality engaging lessons no matter where in the world you are. It's affordable too.

Learn Persian With One-on-One Classes

We provide one-on-one Persian language tutoring online, via Skype. We believe that one-to-one tutoring is the most effective way to learn Persian.

Qualified Native Persian Tutors

Working with the best Persian tutors in the world is the key to success! Our Persian tutors give you the support & motivation you need to succeed with a personal touch.

It's easy! Here's how it works

Request a FREE introductory session
Meet a Persian tutor online via Skype
Start speaking Real Persian in Minutes

Send Email to: info@LearnPersianOnline.com

Or Call: + 1-469-230-3605

40536000R00098

Made in the USA
Middletown, DE
15 February 2017